*A gift for Bert* who has help...

Papa's Neighbors is a fictional story based on the character of the late William McKinley Justice, Pike Co. poet and educator. Written in the same homey style as Mama's Kitchen Window, Mrs. Kinder's book about her mother's character, this 2nd book deals with her father's helping the neighbors in Deep Valley. Mrs. Kinder writes "Mountain Roots" for the Appalachian Express and "Mountain Echoes" for The Pike County News.

"To God be the glory"
Alice J. Kinder

# PAPA'S NEIGHBORS

*Glimpses of Life in the Kentucky Hills*

by
Alice J. Kinder

Beacon Hill Press of Kansas City
Kansas City, Missouri

Copyright, 1979
Beacon Hill Press of Kansas City

ISBN: 0-8341-0581-0

Printed in the
United States of America

## *Dedication*

To
the memory of
my father,

William McKinley Justice,

whose daily steps
in walking the Christian pathway
made him a modern Good Samaritan

## *Contents*

| | |
|---|---|
| 1. The Neighbors of Deep Valley | 9 |
| 2. The Old Log Church on the Hill | 18 |
| 3. Papa's Welcome Doorstone | 23 |
| 4. Papa Seeks a Perfect Church | 28 |
| 5. Papa's Silver Dollar | 39 |
| 6. Papa's Special Day | 44 |
| 7. Stars in Deep Valley | 50 |
| 8. Papa's Special Cross | 60 |
| 9. Someone Knocking at the Door | 64 |
| 10. The Givingest Church Member | 74 |
| 11. Papa's Only Shirt | 82 |
| 12. The Boy Who Became a Methodist Minister | 87 |
| 13. The New Baptist Church on Pinnacle Mountain | 97 |
| 14. The Young Salvation Army Captain | 107 |
| 15. Papa's Graduation | 115 |

# 1

# The Neighbors of Deep Valley

Mama once said that Deep Valley contained the most varied assortment of neighbors to be found anywhere. "And at one time or another, Will," she declared emphatically, "each one has run to you, seeking help in unravelling his skein of problems."

"All people have problems," mused Papa. "And different types of people form a community."

The different types, as Mama well discerned, flocked around Papa almost incessantly. Even before he became a professing Christian the neighbors found their way to our doorstep, or else he walked to theirs to discuss spiritual values or help solve problems.

Naturally, though, after he accepted the Lord as his personal Savior, Papa held more definite ideas on helping people and sharing life's meaningful moments. True and lasting Christianity, he felt, called for belief, faith, and action—a mixture of all three. And daily walking these steps was what counted in life. The ladder to heaven, he asserted, couldn't be built in isolated moments. It must be erected by a succession of everyday chapters.

Considering Papa and his naturally reticent manner, Mama sometimes wondered what he gleaned from the companionship of others.

"How you and Sam Lightner can sit 60 stretched-out moments in complete silence is beyond my womanly understanding," she commented one September day. "Why, Letitia wouldn't continue on speaking terms with me if I clammed up when she came to visit."

A slow smile trailed tentatively from Papa's generous lips as his dreamy, brown eyes observed a pile of hickory nuts. He lifted his right hand to his chin in a thoughtful gesture.

"Sam and I climbed a trail of the mountain in gathering these," he reflected. "God seems inexpressibly close on such heights. Speech is superfluous since the Presence hovers near."

He stopped to examine his next sentence. "God's silence is closer to real being and awareness of life than any words or actions of men. And He speaks to us only when our own soul is silent and free of schedules. Reckon after Sam and I left the heights we still savored the glory up there, where God stands between one and all difficulties."

Such thought constituted a long speech for Papa. More often he was like a child when reprimanded, his lips screwed tightly together while meditating on favorite Bible verses or weighing speculative ideas. Yet when he unloosened the screws from his inner thought, he displayed a wealth of opinions.

"Which merely proves," Mama said in summing up the situation, "that patchwork traits and thoughts churn around in everyone. And after all, why not? It would be rather dull if you knew all the roomy dimensions of everybody's mind. Looking around the bend for unexplored corners makes the view more exciting."

Yes, Papa took his time in speech if he wished to meditate further. But when he knew positively that he was right, he didn't stop for additional thought. Without flinching, he stood bravely for his opinions and immediately acted on them.

More than one of his opinions on what was right revolved around the neighbors and the gradual unfolding of their tangled lives. He tried to understand the individual soul of each neighbor in Deep Valley, since he believed one needed to search with empathy for the real "I's" and "you's" of people in order to help them. Most of all, he tried to help those who'd lost sight of all vision or hope.

"The down-and-outers," Papa would say, "are the very ones requiring a neighborly spirit of communication, since they view only the dirt and despair beneath their feet. If we can show such as these that God really cares, they'll come to know Him as a living reality and lift their faces toward the sun again."

Papa helped many reach for the sunlit rays. He knew that God moves concretely in plain, everyday experiences, and he simply had to share that awareness with others. Christianity was too vital a faith to be hoarded in solitary confinement, he said, and the word "others" faced one squarely when you held faith to the mirror. For him, the word meant the neighbors around him.

Each person's soul groped for someone else's inner thought, he felt, seeking companionship and understanding. Only by becoming acquainted with your neighbor's daily life and his problems could you grow even partially aware of his invisible self. The scrutiny helped a person to understand better his own unseen self then and examine conscientiously his reactions when confronted with difficulties.

"Each of us is a problem. We're reaching for a satisfactory answer to the meaning of existence," Papa once said. "And each deed of ours is linked with the actions of others. Our characters mature or deteriorate through our acts and the activities of others."

One day Sam Lightner called Papa a Good Samaritan. In their conversation across the fence Papa frequently shared with Sam the latest farming ideas from his agricultural magazines. More important, though, he shared truths from the Book that he prized above all others—the one he read through assiduously 17 times.

"Start reading a portion of the Bible each day," Papa advised Sam. "You'll gain further truth with each new reading, as you savor the divine words anew."

Beyond Sam's farm lay Ben Trainer's land. Papa helped Ben straighten out his tangled life and marry Aunt Noreen. Uncle Pettigrew lived near Ben. Next came Dan Bender, who couldn't get ahead; Mama's brother Bartley, who prospered in merchandise; and Nathaniel and Magdalena Lane.

Daddy Lovell, the valley teacher, was sometimes ill with asthma. Papa's intuition led him to check often on Mr. Lovell. Charlie Lennon was our neighbor, and so was poor, disillusioned Milt Tanner, who felt he didn't have a friend in the world until he was converted under Papa's leadership one snowy night in a fodder shock.

Hermann Kiser and his children came to visit us. Then there were the Trelawneys, the Green spinsters, the Howard Tanners with whom Papa shared our orchard, and Tim Malone and his industrious wife. Grandpa Simms often required a helping hand. And sometimes others in our valley needed help.

A variety of peddlers and drummer boys stopped on their way to Lonesome Cove. Since we lived in an isolated

Kentucky mountain area with only two stores, we welcomed travelers with their packs of notions. Stopping overnight and sometimes staying longer, they became our neighbors too.

As a simple layman and a steward of the soil, Papa witnessed about God's love to all who became a part of Deep Valley. Our valley was the loveliest land on earth, so Papa felt. He liked to read the book of James while walking across his wide, fertile acres. Along with James, he believed that faith without works is inert. Believing this, he tried hard to practice the Golden Rule despite the fact that he, like everyone, was endowed with human failings of the flesh.

No, Papa wasn't perfect; he failed at times, the same as anyone else. He could grow angry over little things—such as fitting stovepipes or having to wait while Blarney balked with the plow. Occasionally he grew irritated at Mama's chatter when he wanted to think. And if my brothers and I quarreled over the chores he didn't hesitate to take stern measures, sometimes strapping the innocent in his haste. At rare intervals also, he and certain relatives spoke heated words over trivial differences.

But that was what living energetically amounted to, Papa said—becoming involved in the very core of life. If the core held unsavory seeds, it was up to us to pare away the bad seeds and replace them with more loving and forgiving thoughts. Right actions would then follow, paving the way for improved relationships.

"Christian relationships grow only through living and growing spiritually beside others," Papa asserted, as he rode to church one Father's Day beside Lem Bollen.

That particular Father's Day was a special event in Papa's career of Christian witnessing. And other days set aside to honor fathers were memorable also. Father's Day was ever a special occasion in our household, because we had an upright man to honor and be proud of—a father who believed so steadfastly in God that he wouldn't consider starting the day until he had read his Bible, shared confidences with his Maker, and sought guidance for the schedule ahead.

"God pushes me off in the morning," Papa witnessed to Lem that day. "He guides me in taking my first step each day. Sure, I stumble a lot, but He continues to walk beside me in steadfast companionship. He is always near, whether or not I remember the assurance of His care. And when I falter He beckons me on, one step at a time."

# 2

# The Old Log Church on the Hill

Sitting in the old log church on the highest hill in the Deep Valley community, one could almost reach out to grasp God's hand. His presence seemed to hover near. Maybe that was because the height appeared to edge just within sight of heaven's doorway. Our church on Pinnacle Mountain stood tall and beckoning beneath the azure sky.

The mountain air was clean and fresh and invigorating—different somehow from the atmosphere down the hillside where the houses, barns, and hen houses stood. Clear, sparkling water of a spring-fed stream splashed down over smooth, shiny rocks. Near the stream a toasty-gray, lichen-covered rock cavern towered protectively above the church. Misty driblets of moisture dropped from the damp green moss encircling the rock.

Mama and Papa, both barely 20, were married in the old log church on a March day when the temperature dipped to 10 degrees. Those witnessing the ceremony shivered and huddled close for warmth, while the gusty wind whirled at the cracks in the windowpanes. Just as Papa affirmed his "I do," though, in a clear, positive voice, the sun, hitherto playing hide-and-seek with hovering clouds, poured forth energetically in a radiant gesture of sparkling brilliance.

The next year the church was again the scene of an important event. On a summer day Papa proudly carried his firstborn son, Clayton Raphael, in his arms. After the service, the neighbors flocked around Mama and the new baby while Papa strolled outside with two of the preachers. As usual, they stood discussing scriptural theories and again Brother Dennis asserted that Papa would make a good church member.

Papa wasn't ready to join the Primitive Baptist Church, the only church in our community at that time, though he faithfully attended the services held once a month (the preachers preached elsewhere on other Sundays). Upright in reverent attention, he listened intently to the sermons of three, four, or even five ministers on a particular Sunday.

Despite his respect for spiritual matters, though, Papa didn't feel any urge to join the church. He had read and studied far too widely to accept certain ideas the local ministers held. Above all, he couldn't conform to the intolerant view some held of each other and other churches.

The spring after Clayton's birth two preachers in Lonesome Cove disagreed over some minor issue, and some of those exhorting on sin in Deep Valley shunned each other's company beyond the church door. People took sides with the various preachers, and the controversy lasted for months.

"My concept of God doesn't parallel any of theirs," Papa decided on a Sunday afternoon in November. "Yet both you and I, Betsey, derive a blessing from the services.

Despite its failure, the church keeps spiritual values alive here in our hills."

"Most of our people belong to it," Mama checked her syllables precisely. "Will, perhaps we . . ." Her voice lingered on a wistful note.

Papa sat tall above her. "My God is very real to me," he asserted. "So real that I can't be a hypocrite and join a church that I don't believe in wholeheartedly. The step would be against my principles."

He rose from his chair and looked out the window.

"Betsey, I do wish we had a church with a regular pastor. And Sunday school for the children. I've read that people away from here attend churches where young people have Bible classes."

Both he and Mama looked down at their small son. "Brother Dennis was rather powerful today," Papa admitted then.

"Will," Mama declared impulsively, "let's invite him and the other ministers for dinner next month!"

When the next church time rolled around, Mama cooked a bountiful meal for the preachers and several neighbors. Hurrying about to see that everyone was fed, she enjoyed the juicy compliments on her favorite recipes. Papa sensed a shy pleasure in the company and listened carefully to the varied ideas of the ministers.

He remained unusually silent while a white-haired elder expounded his theories on Revelation.

"The book is a divine ending to the Bible," the preacher finished his discourse. "Say, Will, why don't you ride over to Lonesome Cove next Sunday? After the service you can take dinner with my family."

Papa looked toward Mama. She was well advanced in her second pregnancy. Moreover, the weather might turn bad any time, since Christmas was only a week away.

"Next Sunday is Christmas Eve," he reflected slowly. "And with Betsey's condition . . ."

"We'll come if at all possible," Mama interrupted. "I'm tired of staying cooped up in the house. And the weather is marvelous for this time of year."

The next Sunday she couldn't wait to start for Lonesome Cove. Leaving Clayton with Grandma, she and Papa hurried along the frost-tinseled ground. Above them a gray sky had followed a clear dawn hinting sunlight.

"I don't like this cloudy sky trailing the frost," Papa whispered as they entered the church.

"Nonsense," replied Mama blithely. "You and your weather forecasts!"

After the service, which made both Mama and Papa probe deeper yet into spiritual insights, the sky continued to resemble a thick layer of gray, sheep wool. Concerned over their homeward journey by this time, they regretfully declined the preacher's invitation to dinner. Hurriedly they started back to Deep Valley. Large snowflakes began falling as they neared Pinnacle Mountain. Something else started, too—Mama's labor pains!

"Will, it just can't be!" she cried in terror, bending over her saddle. "It wasn't like this at all with Clayton. It isn't time, Will!"

"Betsey, the snow streams faster now. Can we hurry a mite?"

"I can't go much further, Will. I simply can't!"

"We're nearing the top of the mountain," Papa encouraged her. "And our house is the first at the foot of the hill."

After that they rode in silence until within sight of the old log church at the top of the mountain. And there for the third time they prepared to enter on a momentous occasion!

"We're stopping here, Will," Mama spoke determinedly in a low voice. "We have to. The baby's coming."

"But, Betsey—"

"We're stopping, Will. There's no other way."

Papa didn't take time to step lightly from his horse as usual. He leaped to the ground and reached frantically for Mama. Holding her close, he ran to the porch. He stopped only to untie the string on the door latch.

Inside the room he hastily prepared a bed on a bench with curtains he tore from the windows. He built a fire, drew water from the well, and heated it in the water bucket. For the first and only time then, he helped a baby make its entry into the world!

A few hours later, in the Christmas Eve twilight, Mama and Papa watched the flames from the old Ben Franklin stove swirling around the crack in the stove door. The church inside was all cozy and warm, while the snow outside streamed from the sky in soft, trailing skeins. The horses leaned near the windowpanes, neighing gently.

When Papa went out for more water and coal, he found a little stray puppy in the coalhouse. It followed him in and snuggled near Mama and the baby. A flock of sparrows huddled on the window sill.

Mama looked around the room to savor its shelter and warmth. "Will, it's so comforting and peaceful here in the old log church."

Papa looked down at his wife and new son. Grateful thanksgiving lighted his brown eyes. He reached to tuck his coat and hers more closely about them.

"Betsey, our son is born in a church," he spoke in reverent awe. "Are we still going to name him George for your father?"

Something in Papa's voice linked with Mama's thought. She trailed her finger over the baby's head. "Do you prefer another name?"

"Betsey . . ." Papa searched for words. His right hand reached up to touch his chin in the gesture that he used unconsciously when thoughtful or weighing opinions.

"Well," said Mama, waiting, her blue eyes tender.

"Let's call him John," Papa spoke at last, as he thought of the preaching that day. "John's vision of the isle of Patmos is wondrous beyond earthly thought."

"John he shall be," agreed Mama. "Will," she said gently, "our son could be called to preach someday, you know."

Papa remained quiet after that and presently Mama, very tired, went to sleep. Neither could discern at the time, of course, that John would grow up to be the first pastor in our family.

After that extraordinary Christmas, the years fell quickly from the calendar with busy activities and our family increasing fast. As the years unrolled, Papa and Mama always made time to attend services at the old log church on the hill where they'd spent so many meaningful hours. Still, Papa never got around to joining the Primitive Baptist Church.

"I couldn't possibly do without God," he asserted. "But . . ." His voice, as always then, trailed to the uncertain period linked with suppressed longing.

When the first daughter, Jettie-Elizabeth, was born, she arrived in Mama's bed, to everyone's satisfaction. She died in Mama's bed that same year. This time the Jennings family entered the church on a sad occasion. Four preachers presided at the funeral.

My brother Jim's arrival did much to comfort Papa and Mama. Since Mama had just finished the book of James, she herself decided against using her father's name and named her third son. (Jim's future career, like John's, included pastoring, too.) The next baby, Jerry, was named for Papa's brother at Grandma's request. A fifth son soon followed Jerry.

By this time Mama felt that Papa, in fathering so many sons, deserved one named for him. She chose correctly, everyone agreed, since little Willie looked exactly like Papa with serious, dark brown eyes, a broad forehead, and the same pointed chin held erect in determination. When he learned to walk he walked like Papa, too, stepping energetically toward his destination.

But small William had only begun to walk well when he sickened and died. "Spinal meningitis," was old Doc Wainwright's diagnosis following his hasty trip from Lonesome Cove. Again a funeral was held in the church on the hill.

Like others engulfed in sorrow through separation by death, Papa and Mama felt they would never recover from their heartache. But the priceless cure of time worked on their side.

"And God is ever near," Papa affirmed as always. "We're still in His hands. After all, trouble rarely covers the whole sky. The sun edges out in at least one stream of hope and cheer."

"I'd love to have a daughter," Mama mused wistfully one afternoon. "You see, Will, I may just need feminine companionship for a change someday."

To her surprise, she found that she could halfway smile again.

Papa lifted his thoughtful brown eyes to meet her blue ones. "Yes, a daughter would be a comfort, Betsey."

When the daughter ultimately arrived they named her Alicia Jennifer Jennings. They called me Jenny. Since I completed the family, Mama never did get around to using her father's name.

Down through the years Papa and Mama took us children along to attend services at the old log church on

Pinnacle Mountain. Without warning, then, the place where our family had spent such memorable moments was suddenly erased from our lives. A cloudburst crashed down the hollow near the church one summer day. It demolished the church and flooded Deep Valley.

Two months later another catastrophe struck our family. Our home burned and we lived in the barn several weeks. But God was ever near us through deaths, floods, or fires. His presence was, like the Bible, eternal and never failing.

As we made the barn into a home, we worked together and sensed closer family relationships. Maybe that was because we were continually bumping into one another, or perhaps we were drawn closer because of our loss. Be that as it may, the neighbors seemed closer also since they came calling more than ever while we lived in the barn.

Most of all, though, God came calling 24 hours a day. The communication line between Him and our family was always clear. Not once, when we needed Him, did He send out a busy signal. We dropped the tangles of life in His care and left them there.

Through God's care our faith grew daily. We knew that He would unfold the chapters of our lives as we were able to translate them into the necessary paragraphs. He stood in front of all the tomorrows. Each day, we knew, would confront God before it unraveled for us.

# 3

# Papa's Welcome Doorstone

Papa took great pride in the new house he and the boys built with the help of the neighbors. Under his leadership they cut the logs, hewed the notches, and fitted each cornered end with a creative touch. When the house was finished Papa added the final necessary touch as he placed a huge, flat rock before our front doorway.

Without fail he kept the doorstone whitewashed the year around. The labor proved to be a tremendous task, since an unending stream of visitors traveled across it.

Relatives from both sides of the family came with their children. Sometimes we had every bed in the house occupied and pallets on the floor, while the boys slept frequently in the barn loft. They might as well be boarding out there, Mama remarked once, when we had nine relatives, two peddlers, and a drummer boy staying overnight.

The day after all this company left, Sam Lightner visited us. He wanted Papa to write a deed. He was selling his place and moving to Lonesome Cove.

When they'd finished the paperwork, Sam remarked, "You've been a good neighbor, Will."

Papa cleared his throat to cover his shy embarrassment. "Why, thank you, Sam. If I've been any help, you're more than welcome."

Sam reached for his hat and pressed the fold in its crown. "I remember our talks in the fields," he spoke thoughtfully. "And your reading the Bible here by the hearth. I liked the story about the men who had talents. And the one about the man who helped the robbed fellow."

"That was the parable of the Good Samaritan." Papa looked earnestly at his neighbor. "Sam, I wish you'd read for yourself the stories Jesus told."

"But they don't seem real when I read them."

Outside the door Mr. Lightner paused in his steps. "Your doorstone is a real thing, though. We've discussed a lot of worthwhile points, Will, through my stepping over it."

That night in our devotional hour, Papa sat with his chin propped on his right hand. He stared at his left shoe. "I wish I'd led Sam to see the value of Bible reading," he spoke regretfully.

"You did your best, Will," comforted Mama. "Even Jesus failed at times to reach those nearest Him."

We heard of the Lightners at intervals after that. Mr. Lightner was building up his new farm and clearing more land. He and Letitia managed well in spite of the depression and the fact that nine children now sat around their table. Still considering the family as our neighbors, Papa included them as always in his prayer. Just because they'd moved away was no reason to drop them from our prayer list.

That fall we didn't get a chance to dig our potatoes because someone else dug them instead. Someone raided our hen house, too, and took all the chickens except five banty hens. Many families reported worse thefts. Depression was hard on everyone, Papa declared, but remembering Job he affirmed that we must cling to faith and seek patience in all tribulation.

An October Sunday found Papa pointing out this truth to Milton Tanner. In our old porch swing, the two sat beneath a blue sky dotted with puffs of gray-twirled clouds sailing around in a hopscotch manner. As he surveyed the clouds, Milton spoke heatedly on the thefts in our valley.

"Yes, these are indeed hard times," admitted Papa.

He, too, scanned the sky, then spoke positively. "God isn't a fair-weather god, though. He is one for all seasons. Some good may come out of the evil, despite everything."

Milt smiled quizzically. "Please enlighten me, Will, when such news makes the headlines."

Again he observed the sky. "Well, I only hope no prowler sneaks to my place tonight. Those clouds are scooting around to blow up the very night for a thief's fingers to itch."

A storm developed that night while we visited Grandma. When we returned home we found trees across the road. In the yard we started to step over the doorstone. As Papa held the lantern close we saw someone huddled in a soggy mass. It was Sam Lightner with a swollen bruise on his forehead!

Papa and the boys hastily carried him in. Clayton lighted a fire to dry Sam and his clothes. We sat around the cheerful, butter-and-red flames and listened in wonder to Sam's story.

"I was looking for Letitia's pet cow," he disclosed. "Near a ravine a man with a black cloth over his face rose from the bushes. He started toward me with a club. That was the last I remembered."

"Quite a bump you have there," discerned Papa.

"The clouds had been muddling together. When I came to, the rain had showered down. My watch was gone and so was the one dollar in my pocket."

"This stealing!" exclaimed Mama in the identical tone Mr. Tanner had used earlier.

"I thought I couldn't move at first," continued Sam. "Every movement sent sore trickles seeping through me. And then I remembered your house here by the foot of the hill. If I could make it to your welcome doorstone I'd be cared for, of course."

"Our welcome doorstone!" echoed Mama.

"Yes. I thought of it every step of the way along with the story of the Good Samaritan," replied Sam in a low voice.

"The Good Samaritan?" This time Papa's voice echoed, while his notes dripped with reverence because the words came from the Bible and deserved respect and awe.

"You see, Will, I've been reading the Bible, as you advised me to do."

Papa cleared his throat. He watched the flames spiral up the chimney. Outside, the rain had thinned to a faint mist while the wind sighed only now and then across the window sills. Sam looked toward the window and the darkness. He turned to hold his hands gratefully to the firelight.

"I can't bear malice against the man who robbed me," he thought carefully, "since because of him I came once more to you, Will—a Good Samaritan. The moment I fell out there tonight I knew at last your way was right, the way you trust God and treat others as you would have them treat you."

He observed the bright fire again, then noted the soft glow from our lamp. "Why, Will Jennings, I must be your neighbor still!" he exclaimed in grateful wonder.

Again Papa cleared his throat. "Give God the praise," he answered quietly. "I merely pray each day—and try to follow His directions."

Papa sent a shy, grateful look in Sam's direction. No one had ever called him a Good Samaritan before. His welcome doorstone, however, stood as a witness that he believed and acted along the same route as the unnamed Samaritan who traveled the Jericho road.

# 4

# Papa Seeks a Perfect Church

After Sam Lightner called him a Good Samaritan, Papa began thinking of the church and standing up publicly for the Lord in a different light. Also, some time after that Mama stood on her principles in walking the aisle and joining the Primitive Baptist Church. If one meant to witness for the Lord and the Bible, maybe he should stand upright before the world to assert that he stood for the Christian faith. Still, Papa told Mama firmly that he couldn't join the Primitive Baptists.

He was in a quandary on how to arrange his map of religious faith.

And then one day Rev. Floyd Delaney, a Presbyterian, entered our valley. He came from a group of dedicated Christians up north in Ohio. They planned to start mission Sunday schools in the Kentucky mountains. The Reverend Delaney enlisted Papa's help to build a little mission church down near the mouth of Deep Valley. Papa visited among the neighbors daily to interest them in the new church, and after months of delay the building was ready to spread God's Word.

On a lovely June morning, a foggy gray dawn unrolled a young sky filled with the promise of bright sunlight. As we prepared to attend Sunday school for the first time, my brothers and I bumped into various elbows, with all of us trying to peek into the front hall dresser mirror at once.

In her bedroom Mama used her own mirror for braiding her long brown hair. Papa sang "The Ninety and Nine" on the back porch and used the cracked mirror over the blue and white wash bowl while he shaved. It was a blessing that everyone had taken turns bathing in the washtub out in the smokehouse the night before, or we would never have been ready by nine o'clock.

At precisely nine by Papa's watch we started to Sunday school. Mama didn't see why we had to start so early. However, Papa always liked to be on time. On time for him, and his family, meant stepping over the threshold before anyone else.

And we were on time that morning because no one else had yet stepped through the door when we arrived. The building that Papa had dreamed about and helped build stood on a sloping knoll between two forks of our valley. Its new, white paint glistened in the sun. The new glass windows sparkled with cleanliness. Tall green poplar trees beside the windows provided a colorful contrast to the white paint.

We stood beneath the branches and listened to the singing birds. After what seemed a very long time Rev. Delaney arrived with a young man and his wife.

"This young couple from my church doesn't mind work," he assured us after he'd introduced Mary and Carl Higgins. "That's why they're here working for the Lord. They'll be with you this summer to get the Sunday school started."

We liked Mary and Carl. Mary was a little like Mama with buttery-gold hair and blue eyes. Her laugh tinkled like Christmas bells and she was always smiling. Carl was tall, though not as tall as Papa. His hair was sandy red, his eyes a pale blue. His brown-rimmed glasses made him look distinguished and dignified.

The minister took charge and explained how Sunday school classes were organized. We listened with wonder since we'd never been in such a classroom before. However, after he mentioned some of the stories we would study I didn't feel lost at all. Papa had read the stories of Abraham, Jacob, and David to the boys and me since we were old enough to listen.

Only 10 grownups in Deep Valley, besides Mama and Papa, were present. Rev. Delaney taught the adult class. Carl Higgins taught the boys. And Mrs. Higgins gathered us girls around her.

Later the classes would be divided. The minister asked Papa to teach the adult class on the following Sundays since he must return home. If Mama would help with the girls' class as the attendance grew, perhaps someone would volunteer to teach a division of the boys. Mama's sister, Aunt Noreen, volunteered. She knew plenty about boys' actions, having five boys of her own.

Mrs. Higgins gave my class some pretty colored cards with a picture of Jesus and little children gathered about Him. She taught us to sing "Jesus Loves Me." I'd never heard the song before. I meant to practice singing it every day of my life because it was the loveliest tune I'd ever heard.

That night I asked Papa to sing the song. He and the boys sang with me while Mama played the organ. Papa's strong, resonant voice filled our kitchen and drifted out to the well sweep, the wood block, and the pasture field. Our whippoorwill near the edge of the hillside answered in melodious notes. Mama said she had a certain feeling that Sunday school would be good for everyone.

Our whole family soon became involved with Sunday school work. Mama and Papa studied the Bible and the literature diligently, attempting to become better teachers. And Clayton and John did, too, since they helped with a class of the youngest boys. Jim, Jerry, and I helped them find pictures for their posters. All of us practiced the songs and Bible verses. We never missed a Sunday of attendance except on the fourth Sunday of the month. As Mama and Papa had agreed, that Sunday was reserved for our going to Lonesome Cove to attend the church where Mama had been baptized.

But one fourth Sunday we didn't attend services anywhere. A thunderstorm had caused the creeks to overflow their banks. On the hillside several trees, struck by lightning, blocked our pathway. That Sunday seemed longer than three weekdays woven together.

"It doesn't seem right to stay at home on the Lord's day," mused Mama.

"Why, Betsey," said Papa, "we can worship God right here by the hearth."

He rose to his tall height of six feet and three inches to watch the raindrops spattering hard on the barn roof. "In fact, we always have," he added as an afterthought.

He remained silent several moments, assiduously chewing a toothpick between his strong, white teeth. "Betsey," he resumed the conversation, "that young Carl Higgins is a deep-minded preacher."

Beside her work table, Mama strained the milk in her churn. "I'm glad he's started preaching now in addition to teaching his class," she observed with satisfaction. "It's a comfort to attend real church services along with the Sunday school."

Papa continued to meditate and chew his toothpick.

"Betsey, getting right down to the core of the matter," he reflected, "these Presbyterians like Carl aren't much different in their beliefs from the doctrines in your church."

"*My* church, Will Jennings!" exclaimed Mama. "I just wish that for one time you'd quit saying *your* church with that particular emphasis. No one owns a church, Will. Churches stand for God."

To Mama, the matter was as simple as that. But not to Papa. Because no matter how hard he tried to withhold criticism, he still believed that ministers stressed their own private interpretations on God's Holy Word to the exclusion of other opinions and sometimes, to state the case mildly, he felt that they were wholly wrong. His opinions didn't yet coincide with the ideas they held.

"Yes, Carl preaches a lot like the Baptists," Papa decided. "And he's a thinking man with a college degree. I like his sermons tremendously. Still . . ."

"I know," interrupted Mama, energetically tying a clean cloth over the churn. "You can't join a church that you don't believe in wholeheartedly. You can't give up your cherished ideas. Oh, Will, am I to hear those statements the rest of my life? What are you looking for, Will— a perfect church run by imperfect men, as all men are, including you?" she added a mite tartly.

With an impatient gesture resembling Mama's voice Papa threw the toothpick flat on the table. He turned abruptly and left the room.

For three days an edgy coolness drifted between my parents. The coolness continued until Tuesday around five o'clock when we heard a knock on the door. It was Ben Trainer. He said that Carl Higgins was sick and Mary was extremely worried about him.

Papa reached hurriedly for his hat. "I must go to Carl. It will be too late to return home, Betsey, so I'll stay in town tonight."

"Oh, Will." Mama lifted her blue eyes, filled with concern, to his. "Be careful, dear. I never feel easy with you gone for the night."

A small, plump figure less than five feet tall, she looked up at Papa, He hugged her tightly. The last cool mist between them evaporated.

Carl Higgins remained ill almost two weeks and Papa visited him at every available opportunity. "One thing about your papa," Mama declared one day, "he never fails to go when someone needs him."

She turned to latch the door. "You see, he's just so perfect in almost every way—and seeks perfection in others." She sighed deeply as she reached for her sewing basket.

A few days later Papa sighed, too. Or rather, he returned home as if he were sighing inside. He entered the door slowly, holding his right hand up to his chin in the old nervous gesture. But only after he had sat silently several minutes, did he confide in us.

He cleared his throat. "Um-umph. Yes, Carl is improving," he spaced his syllables with precision. "Still, he isn't yet on his running feet. Mary wants you to send a pot of your special vegetable soup, Betsey."

He remained silent again, staring hard at his left shoe.

"Of course." Mama then waited, since she knew that after Papa's silences he always came up with something unique or out of the ordinary.

This time, however, the announcement was one we wouldn't have imagined in five decades. "Betsey," Papa at length spoke bravely, "Carl wants me to preach for him on Sunday."

If Papa had proclaimed that our house would grow wings and fly to Venus we wouldn't have been more overwhelmed! Papa preaching from a pulpit! "Oh, no!" cried Mama distractedly.

In her apprehension she then uttered the first words that came to mind. "I never thought to see the day when I'd become a preacher's wife!"

Papa slowly lifted his anxious brown eyes to hers. When he saw that she wasn't teasing him, he relaxed his huge knuckles that he'd been twisting nervously. "Betsey, what . . . am I . . . to do?"

His voice was like a child's, seeking direction.

"Oh, Will," said Mama gently. Her mind churned with thoughts that sought direction also.

Just how, she wondered, could Papa preach when he criticized the preachers so? Such a paradox, she thought. He loved God and his Bible more reverently than anyone she knew; he loved to attend church and listen to sermons. And yet he insisted always in looking for a perfect minister and a flawless church. From her womanly insight and her certain feeling, she knew he would never find either.

But now he had been asked to preach himself and he wasn't even a church member! He'd never be given that privilege in the Baptist church, Mama knew, unless he'd been baptized, all six feet and three inches of him, completely in the water. These Presbyterians who'd entered our valley were organized rather queerly, she sometimes thought.

"Will," she spoke determinedly, as she rose to the occasion, "you're starting ideas for your sermon tonight. And you will preach from that pulpit on Sunday!" Her voice held courage sufficient for the two of them.

Despite her assertion, however, Papa didn't reach out immediately to accept a helping of her courage. Never yet had he broken a promise, though. "That's just the trouble," he sighed. "I can't say no to anyone. If only I hadn't promised Carl!"

"Stop brewing trouble. I have faith in you—enough to be shared by both of us," Mama said encouragingly.

The next morning Papa accepted a portion of her faith. On using it, he discovered it could grow sufficiently for him to mix ideas for his sermon. He then became so engrossed with the mixture that he tackled the task with enthusiasm. After all, if he truly intended to preach he might as well be a success. Which was a sane way to view the matter, Mama agreed placidly.

"When I start a job I like to see it through," Papa asserted with pride. "I'll mix my ideas well, center them on a definite theme, and stick to it. I don't like sermons that wander aimlessly and aren't tied together."

"Um," replied Mama, as she added salt to her soup mixture.

After some meditation, Papa chose the topic, "Forgiving One's Neighbor." He wrote all afternoon and came up with some of the most beautiful ideas we'd ever heard. Mama, the boys, and I listened to them while Papa preached to us as he practiced his sermon. Then Sunday rolled around, and it was time for him to preach in church!

We got up earlier than usual and arrived at the church door 15 minutes before nine. Papa hurried about in his important role as he straightened the seats and checked the hymnbooks.

Mama adjusted the pin in her new hat and stood with pride as she looked toward the pulpit. "He'll do well," she observed confidently. "I thought he'd be nervous, but just look at your papa."

By that time people were streaming through the door. Word had spread that Will Jennings would preach that day, and many who'd never before entered the new Presbyterian church came especially to hear him.

"If Will's taking up sermonizing, I may just spend my Sundays here," Dan Bender told Mama. "Of course I'm not in the knack of attending church anywhere."

Mama lifted her left eyebrow. But then playing to

perfection the role of a pastor's wife, she overlooked her usual thought on Dan's inertia and gave him a warm smile. Surely, with everyone's faith in him, Papa would do well. She lifted her bright face to the pastor-of-the-day, sharing an optimistic smile with him. After all, her certain feeling rarely failed.

After Sunday school the opening song for church was a wonderful inspiration. Papa's voice rang vibrant with feeling as he proclaimed the assurance of God's love. In prayer, too, his voice carried conviction as he thanked God for all blessings and divine care.

But alas, when he lifted his face for the sermon, Mama's certain feeling left her stranded in disbelief. For Papa hadn't uttered two sentences when he stuttered, turned as white as the new paint on the walls, help up his right hand toward his chin, looked down at his left shoe—and stumbled from the pulpit.

We were never so humiliated in our lives! But then outside the church everyone clustered about us, offering consolation. They wanted so desperately to help that the Jennings family just had to accept their condolences.

"Think nothing of it, Will," Nathaniel Lane spoke heartily. "You know more words than anyone in these parts, including that college man, Carl Higgins, because you read so much. As for me, I'd be tongue-tied before a crowd, too."

One after another then reminded Papa how he'd helped with their problems. "Why, your helping me, Will, is all the sermon I need from you or anyone," Tim Malone assured him.

After that Papa, still pale and nervous, smiled rather weakly. Gradually he began to feel better as he observed how his friends still rooted for him, despite the fact that he'd failed completely and deprived them of a Sunday sermon. Since they so readily forgave him, he decided that they didn't particularly need his sermon after all.

At home Papa stood tall again beneath his own roof. With no apparent effort he confided to his family how he felt about the one occasion when he failed miserably in a task he undertook.

"As long as I live," he stated emphatically, "I'll never criticize a preacher as I've done in the past. I still have much praying to do on that score before I'll feel wholly forgiven."

He stopped and straightened his shoulders.

"If a man can stand on his feet long enough to provide any sermon at all, then he's a man called of God with words worth listening to," Papa spoke his conviction. "And as for opinions, God doesn't mean for us to grasp the same ones, I suppose, else He wouldn't have arranged our minds in such contrasting departments. Opinions will sift around and clash with each other right up to the Judgment Day."

"Oh, Will," said Mama softly. She was so grateful that she dripped happy tears on the raspberry pie.

The next Sunday Carl Higgins was back in the pulpit to do his own preaching. His words made God's love shower right down on all of us. Papa sat meditating, wholly absorbed in Carl's meaningful ideas.

When the invitation was given he walked slowly forward. Yet he spoke no word of testimony. Only when we reached home did he testify to his family. He then used practically the same words Mama had used.

"I simply had to walk that aisle," Papa confided. "The merciful love God has given me mingled inside me, and I couldn't do anything else. Beside such love, principles didn't matter any more. I forgot them completely and thought only of God's mercy and love in dying for my sins. Now I know what His forgiving grace means."

No, Papa never found a perfect church nor a perfect

pastor. Perfection isn't possible in humanity or in earthly tasks performed by man. But he came to know that God's love is greater than all people and their opinions, all churches and their differences. The important thing was to find a personal relationship with God through Jesus Christ.

Papa knew at last, the glorious, shining truth of God's love and found that the act of committing one's life to Him can bring peace to one's soul.

# 5

# Papa's Silver Dollar

After Papa testified publicly that he had truly been born again, he started a Bible study in our home. There was no set time for everyone to attend. The neighbors just "dropped in" when it was convenient for them. Mama didn't seem to mind having her schedule interrupted. And Papa didn't trouble himself over schedules. Rather, he gloried in minds meeting and soaring through growing, active, spiritual education.

Papa had always attended to the spiritual education of his four sons and only daughter. But after he stood publicly for Christ, he adhered more strictly to God's principles and worthwhile character traits in training us.

As he stood tall by the mantel one October day, he opened the doorway to our chiming clock. Carefully he reached for his silver dollar. Beside him Jim, his eyes shining with achievement, waited expectantly.

"Yes, Jim," said Papa, "it's your turn to own the dollar for a week."

On various occasions each of my brothers and I had held the honor. To attain the status we'd struggled with difficulty to grow tall inside and nourish the small virtues hidden within us.

"Virtues lie waiting to be developed in everyone," explained Papa. "Their growth helps one feel clean inside and adds to stature in climbing character steps."

The person who most fully developed his virtues in measuring up to the 10 rules for growing character in the Jennings family was the one who claimed the honor of owning the dollar.

Papa set great store on the dollar that had been in our family half a century. More important, though, he cherished the development of character belonging to his children.

On Monday morning, just before we started to school, Jim proudly surveyed the silver dollar again. Happily he eased it into the right pocket of his jeans. Taking care of the dollar was one of the points which went along with the ownership. The action involved the acceptance of responsibility, a word one couldn't neglect in developing the kind of character Papa desired for us.

At recess I held the dollar for Jim while he played handsprings. As I held it carefully, I knew that he depended on me and I was responsible for its safekeeping. Just before he came for his possession, I let Sadie Kiser admire its shining surface. Her little brother Tony nearby gazed at it as though it were a Christmas present.

"Oh, Jenny," cried Sadie, "I've never seen a silver dollar before!" The Kisers, new in our valley, lived in a tiny house near the fork of the creek.

"Sister," said Tony, "it shines like Mama's eyes used to do—before she got sick."

At noon Jim's best friends clustered around him, asking to hold the dollar. He permitted them to do so, again sensing exhilaration in the ownership. But that afternoon my brothers and I walked home in a sad procession. Papa's silver dollar was missing!

As we neared our gateway, the five of us crept tentatively toward the house. There was something that had to be done, and all dreaded the ordeal. Of course Jim, accepting the responsibility that went along with the ownership of the dollar, would speak first. Yet as past owners, the rest of us couldn't forget a special rule involved in growing tall inside—the rule of our loyalty to each other. It was our duty to stick by Jim when he confessed the tragic event to our parents.

When he heard the confession, Papa stared intently at our chiming clock. "Nothing is gained by wasting time in regret over past errors," he said. "Confessing them and praying about them is the only way out."

Placing God first in one's life and holding communion with Him was the first rule for developing character, Papa always said. Putting others first and yourself last was the second rule. The acceptance of responsibility followed, and then came the virtue of loyalty. Using time well was rule number five.

After Papa reminded us of the fifth rule, we wasted no further time in mourning our loss. Rather, the next day we made inquiries and searched the school premises. Despite our efforts, though, we failed to find the dollar; nor did we discover a single clue.

Late Wednesday night someone knocked on our front door. Hermann Kiser stood on the threshold. "It's Lizzie!" he cried brokenly. "She's taken worse."

Without delay Papa and Mama hurried home with Mr. Kiser. His wife died that night. The funeral was held on Saturday.

On Saturday night, again Papa stood near our clock. But at that hour, the usual one for proclaiming the next winner of the silver dollar, no fortunate name was announced. Instead Papa reached thoughtfully for the Bible.

He read several verses on the value of worthwhile toil. Laboring industriously was our sixth rule for nurturing character. And then came the discipline of improving our minds and being grateful for blessings.

Despite the loss of our dollar, I felt thankful indeed that night as our family sat cozily by the hearth. I thought of Mrs. Kiser's funeral and remembered Sadie and little Tony, left now without a mother. A timid knock interrupted my thoughts.

Mama opened the door. She discovered the two Kiser children huddled together.

"We've come . . ." began Sadie. Her sad, young eyes stared miserably at the floor.

"Why, come in, children," Mama invited warmly, placing an arm around each of them.

"We've come . . ." began Sadie once more, still not lifting her eyes.

"Here," said Tony, as he reached a small, thin hand toward Jim. "Here's your silver dollar."

"I didn't mean to steal it!" cried Sadie convulsively. "But it was so bright and shining, lying near your book. You bent to look in your desk just as I passed by. I meant to return it after . . ."

"We wanted Mama to see something pretty once more before she died," Tony explained quietly.

"But she didn't get to see it," Sadie confided brokenly. "She was too sick when we got home from school."

"I carried it home in my pocket," confessed Tony. "So I'm to blame as much as Sister is." He stood bravely near Sadie, attempting to wink back the misty dew in his eyes.

Papa laid a gentle hand on the boy's head. "Honesty," he began, as he explained the ninth rule on our list for growing tall inside.

"Here, Tony." Jim held out his handkerchief. "Don't feel too badly." Forgiving others was the tenth rule. Again Jim, practicing the rules, proved himself worthy.

In a simple manner Papa outlined the plan for growing straight inside so that one might live fully the Christian life intended by God.

"Placing God first in one's life is the first step," he explained simply. "If we remember that, we may be sure the other chapters of living will fit in their proper corners."

The two children listened quietly as they attempted to understand. "I'd sure like to own the silver dollar for a week," sighed Tony at the end of the explanation.

And he did the very next week. That was the beginning of our sharing the dollar with the other children in Deep Valley. From that time on Papa included them also in his plan for helping us all grow tall inside.

"The development of character traits isn't to be hoarded for one family alone," he decided that Saturday night. "We parents must work together to nurture worthwhile traits for all."

After that Clayton and John, Jim and Jerry, and I didn't own Papa's silver dollar so often. But somehow, sharing it with others proved wholly rewarding and satisfactory—which was all part of the climbing in building character steps.

# 6

# Papa's Special Day

The sun edged over the eastern hill in a tentative gesture of buttercup loveliness. I beheld the glory part the curtain of fog, pushing its gray spirals aside. The day was beginning precisely like the Easter dawn at the sunrise service, all full of hope and promise.

The Father's Day ahead included happy moments to savor. As I watched the buttery sun melt across the sky, I listed them anew in anticipation.

Around the breakfast table we'd sing Papa's song, and after the blessing he would open his presents. I remembered the five handkerchiefs I'd hemmed for him. Clayton had a new white shirt awaiting our father. John had bought a shirt too, a plaid work shirt. The boys had saved money they'd made in helping Grandpa Simms clear his new ground. Jim and Jerry had used coins they'd saved from selling their pig to buy socks. With a portion of the egg money, Mama had laid away a new pair of shoes.

The presents would please Papa mightily, of course.

Already I could visualize his eyes lighting with wonder and love for us. The glow would last all the time we prepared for church and later, too, while we listened to the sermon. We'd come home then and climb Pinnacle Mountain for our picnic.

That afternoon Papa would read about the fathers of faith in the Bible. As he read about Abraham, Jacob, and Moses, I could almost see the patriarchs lifting our gate latch. Listening to his voice that soared up and then swooped down in just the right places, I would know that the reason Papa possessed so much love in his heart was because he, like those fathers of old, depended daily on his Heavenly Father for guidance.

Mama, too, depended on God for guidance in her daily tasks. Now that she had left the Primitive Baptist Church and joined the Presbyterians, like Papa, the two acted with accord on the same Christian team.

"Fry Papa and the boys two eggs as usual," she directed, while I helped in the kitchen.

Beyond the door I suddenly heard screaming down at the Malone house. "Mama, there's something wrong at the Malones!"

We hurried outside. "Will," said Mama, as she saw Papa near the barn, "did you hear that?"

"Betsey, I'll go right now. Someone needs help."

Papa hurried down the road. The two older boys followed him.

"Wait a bit for the egg frying," Mama said. "They like their eggs hot."

"Mama," called Jerry from the porch after we'd waited long in suspense, "I see John coming back!"

My second brother entered the yard. "Tim Malone didn't come home last night," he said. "Stephen fears he may be drowned in Shelton River."

"I heard the creek chugging in the night," Mama remembered. "And rain drenching the roof."

I hadn't heard the rain at all. Only at dawn did I observe it had fallen. That was why the sun was so glorious this morning, all wreathed in smiles of hope and promise. Sunlight rays always shone more radiantly after a stormy night. Surely tragedy couldn't happen on such a lovely day—especially an event that would hurt Stephen Malone!

"Papa and Clayton will eat with Stephen," John told us. "Then they'll hurry down to Shelton Town. I'll bring Timmy up here."

"Was that Timmy screaming?" asked Mama.

"Yes. He heard Lem Bollen telling Stephen about their father."

"The child always set such store by his papa," reflected Mama, then remained silent a long moment.

I thought of little five-year-old Timmy and again of Stephen, tall and sturdy like Clayton. When I returned to the kitchen I'd almost forgotten it was Papa's Special Day. I remembered then and sensed self-pity, thinking how our day was now ruined.

Just as quickly, though, I grew ashamed of myself. Why, Stephen and Timmy might not even have a father now. And they'd had no mother since she'd died of pneumonia.

That Sunday, while the men dragged Shelton River, I let little Timmy play with the kittens and took him to see the chickens. By nightfall we still had learned no further news of Mr. Malone. The body was not found until Tuesday afternoon.

Stephen and Timmy remained at our house the rest of the week. Because of the grief, any mention of celebration seemed out of place. We hadn't yet brought out the presents.

By Saturday morning, though, I could wait no longer. "Mama," I began when Papa left for town, "may we have Papa's Special Day tomorrow?"

A speculative look rose in her blue eyes. "Go find Clayton," she directed.

The two discussed preparations. Yet before deciding definitely they explained our family celebration to Stephen. Mama asked if he would mind our proceeding with the plans.

He hesitated the wisp of a second. "Why, that will be wonderful," he answered quietly. "Would you mind if I get Mr. Will something, too?" he asked shyly then. "You see, he's been like a—father to Timmy and me."

His serious gray eyes filled with gratitude. Except for Clayton, my favorite brother, I knew Stephen Malone was the most handsome and the smartest boy in the world. He'd taken turns with Clayton in carrying my books home from school, and he showed me how to divide the difficult spelling words into syllables. Daddy Lovell, our teacher, said he couldn't manage without Stephen to help us younger pupils.

"Go right ahead, Son," Mama answered Stephen, addressing him as if he were one of her own boys.

On Sunday morning then, once more the sun splashed forth in beauteous splendor. By this time we had seven presents, since Stephen had bought two pairs of socks. Again I rose to help Mama.

"Fry two eggs for all the menfolk," she directed as usual.

We prepared oatmeal, fried apples, smoked bacon, gravy, and eggs. Mama set the big platter of eggs on the table just as Papa came from the barn.

He saw the presents piled high by his chair. His eyes grew tender with wonder and love. John gave the signal and we sang the song Mama had written in a moment of inspiration.

"Happy Special Day, dear Papa," we sang happily.

When Papa opened the gifts Timmy watched in wonder. "Is it Christmas?" he asked, his round, blue eyes dangling two question marks.

"No, Timmy, we're celebrating Papa's Special Day," explained Clayton.

"We give presents to Papa because we love him," Jerry said.

Timmy left his chair and ran to Papa. "I love you, too, Mr. Will, but I don't have anything to give you except me."

The atmosphere halted to a sudden stillness, so still you could almost hear the morning glories growing near the windowpanes. Mama's eyes grew misty and Papa held the child close.

"I guess you don't need another boy, though." Timmy's voice ended on an apprehensive note as he looked around at my four brothers.

Papa smoothed Timmy's blonde curls. "But I do need another boy. In fact, I need exactly two other boys, a little one and a big one." He turned to Stephen.

Stephen, his gray eyes serious, met Papa's glance squarely. He ran his long, slender fingers through his corn-tassel hair. "Why, Mr. Will—" His voice faltered as he looked around our kitchen. "Of course, Timmy and I have no place to go just now. That is, no home where anyone really wants us."

"You need a little boy?" asked Timmy, as he placed a small hand on Papa's big one.

"I need a little boy," asserted Papa firmly. "And a big one," he added, once more turning to Stephen.

"Why, Mr. Will," Stephen said again.

He stopped to look at both Mama and Papa. "I'll enter high school in the fall," he told them. "But if you could look after Timmy—"

His voice trailed in wonder at the generosity of my parents.

Sitting between Stephen and Clayton, I laid my hand on Stephen's arm. From his tall height he turned to smile at me. His gray eyes held a glad thanksgiving look mingled with his quiet, serious glance.

"It's good to be part of a family again, Little Sister," he said gently.

"Oh, Stephen!" I said.

When he used the boys' pet name for me, little joy bells rang deep inside me. Why, I'd rather have Stephen Malone for a new brother than anyone else in the world. And little Timmy, too, of course. Surely no other girl in Deep Valley would now be so rich as I, with six wonderful brothers to call her own!

I looked at Papa, happy that he had sufficient helpings of love for two additional sons, a big one and a little one.

"Your papa has a roomy kind of love," Mama reflected softly, looking around at all her boys and me.

# 7

# Stars in Deep Valley

We had a marvelous time that summer with Stephen and little Timmy sharing our home. Stephen and the three older boys helped Papa hoe the newly plowed fields. Jerry and I helped Mama and took Timmy along when we fed the chickens and ducks, gathered eggs, or carried in wood. It was a new experience having a brother smaller than myself, one for whom I could invent new stories and games.

When autumn came, Stephen started to school in town. He boarded at the principal's house and did janitorial jobs at school. In this way he was able to buy books, school supplies, and clothes for himself and Timmy.

Clayton had also enrolled in the big high school four miles from Deep Valley. He stayed with our uncle at the edge of town. With both Clayton and Stephen gone, our house seemed lonesome. The Friday nights when they came home were happy hours to anticipate all week. We could hardly wait for the boys' arrival.

Yet the rest of us had lives of our own to live. Mama stayed busy with household chores and the care of little Timmy. Papa had done some teaching through the years in addition to farming. Now he farmed and did substitute teaching as well. He studied his Bible and visited the neighbors to witness of God's love.

That winter we learned a new song, "Will There Be Any Stars in My Crown?" Pastor Horne, who had been our minister since Carl Higgins left for foreign mission work, sang it one Sunday two weeks before Christmas. The next day Papa sang the tune while he milked the cows and mended fences. Mama hummed it as she churned the butter and mended the boys' socks. And I sang the words while pasting Shirley Temple pictures in my scrapbook.

As I thought of stars, I remembered how Grandfather Jennings talked about Venus, Betelgeuse, Arcturus, and Antares. But the stars in the song stanzas weren't the kind you could see in the sky.

"The kind of stars the songwriter meant deals with unselfish acts performed for others," Papa explained.

Just then Nathaniel Lane knocked on our door. Papa and he began studying Daniel together, while I ran to Grandma's old discarded sofa in the little lean-to room off our kitchen to paste more pictures in my scrapbook.

Marveling over the loveliness of my golden-haired idol, I tried to imagine what the life of a beautiful little movie star was like. As I thought of my plain, freckled face and straight, brown pigtails, I couldn't visualize the picture. People like Shirley Temple were admired and famous not only for their looks but for their performances which gave pleasure to many people.

The word "performances" had proved a difficult one for me, but with the help of Papa and Stephen I'd added it to my vocabulary notebook. The collected syllables involved deeds and the actions of people, Papa said. The word didn't apply solely to persons in the entertainment world, he'd said firmly.

"Because all of us perform daily by putting our thoughts into action and bringing them to fulfillment," he pointed out.

I thought of the neighbors around us and their activity. We could never have a Shirley Temple, but just possibly we did have stars in our valley after all, people who in their day-by-day living gave pleasure and satisfaction to others.

Now take old Charlie Lennon, for instance, the owner of two huge, brown bay horses. He dwelt alone, a recluse in his tiny shack. No, he wasn't a bachelor since he'd married when he was a good-looking young man, Mama said.

I wondered how any person, just anyone mind you, could ever have considered Charles Lennon handsome enough to marry him. Age alone couldn't change people that much. But knowing Mama and how her opinions almost invariably proved correct, I permitted the matter to pass.

A bristly, red beard and a drooping, down-at-the-mouth mustache covered the skinny face of the owner of the bays. His overalls, rarely clean and never ironed, bulged out at the sides with tobacco twists. A bent-billed cap, bleached by the sun and rain, perched on his straggly red hair. His long, ungainly feet shuffled along in ancient shoes that looked as if they'd been stored in the attic for years.

Time and again I'd heard Mama remark that it was no wonder Minerva Lennon swished him out of the house along with the dust on her broom after five years of marriage. He'd just drifted into the ultimate state of non-caring about his appearance. No, they never divorced since Minerva, searching her Bible for an answer, couldn't come to a clear-cut decision. Instead, she continued to live in their big farmhouse, while Charlie threw up a shack to shelter him.

Twice a day Minerva cooked hot meals for him. When they were ready he knocked on her door to collect the savory food. He then ambled back to his one room down by the garden where he dined alone.

For three seasons out of the year practically everyone shunned Charlie Lennon's uncouth appearance. But when springtide neared and shy violets warily opened their tender-hued eyes, then the masculine population remembered Charlie. Or, to be more accurate, they recalled his useful bays. With the depression whittling possessions away, many had sold their stock and now owned no horses to plow with.

"Say, Charlie," a neighbor might call on a March afternoon, while the wind housecleaned the winter mud away, "will you be using both horses tomorrow? I'd like to borrow one."

"Well—" Charlie took his time in speech now that his niche in society had risen again, "I guess not. Had meant to plow my potato patch, but that shoulder of mine is triggering my nerves. Howard Tanner is going to plow with Whittier so you may as well take Longfellow." (He'd named the horses after hearing papa read from the American poets.)

As for pay, Charlie didn't ask—nor did anyone offer—a cent for the loan of the horses. Surly and unapproachable as a persimmon in early September was old Mr. Lennon for three-fourths of the year. But with spring's debut his mustache turned triumphantly up like a canoe and he grudgingly emitted a grimace which could almost have been called one-third of a grin.

Yes, for one brief period each year Charlie Lennon could be called a star in our valley, I decided, since his performance in making the bays available for plowing was necessary and gave satisfaction to an audience.

I wiped the paste from my scrapbook and saw Kate Rankin coming to visit Mama. Why, Kate might well be a star also.

As for her popularity, when the frogs croaked in belching hiccups down by the creek in our deep coves, a group of ladies beat a path to Kate's garden. They came to share her patch of winter turnip greens. She could have luck with them when their own drooped at the first frost or failed to resurrect themselves with the return of spring.

"The seed I sowed in August didn't come up, Kate," others complained. "How do you always manage to have such uncommon good luck with your greens?"

Kate, bustling about in a starched, embroidered, white apron, adjusted her perky dust cap at an attractive angle. As the star who knew more than anyone else about the art of producing turnip greens, she welcomed all to her garden, chatted affably, and gleaned the latest gossip in exchange for her greens.

I pasted another picture and watched Papa and Nathaniel, each with a Bible on his lap. Why, Nathaniel was a star also, since his labor provided enjoyment for others. Apparently he'd been elected to raise strawberries for our community and some people over in Lonesome Cove, because persons from both places suddenly evinced a longing for the juicy fruit around the middle of May. Without apology, a line of berry lovers flocked to his strawberry patch, seemingly unaware of the work necessary to span the gap between the setting of plants and the ripe fruit.

"A number of leisurely people consider his berry field community property," Mama had once observed.

Papa, near the window just then, noted five persons on their way to Nathaniel's. "Why, how can they think otherwise since he welcomes everyone like prodigal sons? If someone remembers to offer pay he tells them to go along and buy the children candy."

"Well, Magdalena Lane doesn't allow her generosity to flow in that channel," Mama had retorted emphatically. "She said yesterday she'd be glad to see the berry season end. She can't get a moment's rest for the creaking of the gate latch. You see, only a few people remember to bring their own cookers for the berries."

I didn't have time to think of other stars just then, for Mama wanted me to watch Timmy while she prepared supper. I left my scrapbook reluctantly, still absorbed with ideas woven around the word "stars." Words were useful in more ways than one, I knew by this time, since they could be molded to suit a variety of meanings. Perhaps that was the reason for Papa's insistence that each of us keep a vocabulary notebook and use the words in conversation.

As I played checkers with Timmy, I permitted myself at last then to dwell on what had lain deep in my subconscious all the time. I'd only been entertaining myself with thoughts about stars. Deep inside I'd been longing for a Shirley Temple doll and trying to visualize how I would feel with such a marvelous possession.

"We'll have a mighty slim Christmas this year," Papa had decided a few weeks before. "The depression has hurt everyone, of course."

When he'd said that, I observed the lines of anxiety in his broad forehead and noted gray hairs for the first time in his brown hair. I knew I couldn't ask for such a luxury as a Shirley Temple doll. Still, I couldn't help dreaming of the unattainable vision.

The next week Mama began preparations for Christmas. Timmy and I cracked nuts while she selected her favorite cake recipes. When a knock sounded at the door, she opened it to find Kate Rankin dropping in for another visit.

Before Kate left she disclosed the latest gossip. Hermann Kiser, now that his wife had been dead a considerable spell, had knocked on Minerva Lennon's door to pass the time of day. Of course Minerva, still married to Charlie and always stepping erectly by her strict Baptist doctrine, wouldn't stoop to listen to his advances. Nevertheless, talk had been swinging around.

"When you consider all aspects of the case, though . . ." Kate adjusted her dust cap and permitted a speculative gleam to grow in her bright sparrowlike eyes. "Well, really, Minerva and Charlie haven't actually lived together for 15 years."

That afternoon the first heavy snow of the season showered down. I watched the large white flakes molding a blanket on the lawn and remembered that Kate had spoken about the Green spinsters also. She said Eliza had been swamped with sewing for several days now.

I thought of little Eliza Green with the broken back and the wrenlike, gentle face. Evidently she had been chosen by popular consent to sew for the neighborhood. Proud of the fact that she could look at a particular fashion in the catalog and cut an identical one, Eliza sewed constantly.

Admiration such as, "Why, I couldn't cut and sew like that to save my life," was a skimpy reward, really, but it was enough for meek little Eliza. Some persons remembered to pay her, since she and her sister needed the money. Yet many collected their sewing free and even expected her to furnish the thread!

Why, Eliza Green must be a star in our community, I decided, since new apparel was a pleasure and necessity for all.

Two snowflakes clung together as a pair and I recalled

kind old Mr. Peers, the community cobbler. Papa visited him often and read the Bible to him. Despite his failing eyesight he mended many shoes without pay. Such action surely made him a star on earth. Undoubtedly it would count also for stars in the crown he'd wear in heaven. Kate had told Mama that Mr. Peers, like Eliza, had been busy, too. Mr. Peers and other neighbors in our valley worked hard to help people, I knew.

Next morning the fluffy white snow decorated every tree in Deep Valley. Mama continued her baking. Helping her beat the batter, I could hardly wait for Clayton and Stephen to come home. I awaited eagerly also our Christmas program at the schoolhouse. With my pigtails hidden beneath Jim's cap, I was to be the little shepherd boy.

The boys came home on the 23rd. The next day all of us rode down to the schoolhouse in the new sled Papa had made and to which the boys attached tinkling bells.

Everyone agreed that the program was a success. But the crowning act of the get-together came when we were informed that all present would receive a gift! We could hardly believe the glad tidings, since our teacher had said that considering the lean months and all, we wouldn't draw names this year.

In a secret-Christmasy manner, then, Eliza Green, Kate Rankin, Nathaniel Lane, and old Mr. Peers walked outside to their sleds. They beckoned us to follow, and we stood there as a group in the snow.

Eliza Green, surely spending weeks at her machine, had made handkerchiefs for the men, gay pin cushions for the women, rag dolls for the girls, and stuffed rabbits for the little boys. Kate handed a jar of her canned greens to every adult; she gave a small jar of homemade cookies to each child. Nathaniel Lane gave a pint jar of strawberry preserves to both young and old.

The show fell in flaky tendrils as Mr. Peers reached

beneath a heavy quilt in his sled. Hidden there lay a vast array of mended shoes. He had managed to secure from each of us two shoes needing repair. With painstaking care he'd mended them free as Christmas presents. In the sole of each right shoe were labels containing Bible verses.

Standing together in the snow, we attempted to convery our appreciation. All words seemed inadequate. Again I learned a vital point about words. As lovely and as full of meaning as Papa made them, feelings ranked above syllables.

Feelings certainly ranked first when we looked up to see the pair walking toward us! Of all things, Charlie Lennon, dressed in a new suit, a white shirt, a new black hat and shoes, entered the school yard. He gently held the arm of his wife, Minerva. Kate whispered to Mama that he'd heard of Mr. Kiser's attempt to court Minerva and had taken the correct procedure to move back to his big farmhouse.

Charlie had no present to give; that is, he'd have none until the spring season came. Yet everyone agreed that the best gift he could offer in the wintry cold was the renewal of his marriage contract.

At home that night I meditated again on the different meanings around the word "stars." From the window seat I gazed up at the stars glowing brightly, now that the clouds had cleared, and searched for the Christmas star. I couldn't find it, but inside I sensed a warm, shining Christmas spirit, knowing I'd discovered something else more real instead.

Deep Valley was the most marvelous neighborhood in the world, I decided because of the special altruistic (a new word Papa had taught us the day before) star-people living among us—the neighbors who, through loving labor and at a sacrifice to themselves, provided joy for others. More than likely they didn't stop to consider that their actions were embroidering stars in their heavenly crowns. But that was what Papa had meant all the time, of course.

I decided it had been the loveliest Christmas Eve we'd ever known and I had forgotten completely about the unreachable Shirley Temple doll.

On Christmas morning, then, little surprise bubbles floated in my throat. For beside my stocking I found a present wrapped in white tissue paper from Clayton and Stephen—a beautiful, golden-haired, Shirley Temple doll! The two had sold magazine subscriptions to get her for me.

As I looked up at my favorite brother and the tall young man whom we considered as our adopted brother, again I sensed that words were inefficient at certain golden moments. In that instant I forgot every appropriate word in my vocabulary notebook. My pigtails swinging, I ran to hug them both and they understood the meaning back of what I felt.

I named my beautiful doll Star, rather than Shirley. I loved her dearly, but not more than I cherished Eliza, the rag doll given me by Eliza Green.

# 8

# Papa's Special Cross

As a rule, Papa didn't mind going out of his way to help people. He said that was the meaning of Christianity—going the second mile. Quite often he walked the second mile. And sometimes even the third or fourth.

Every other Saturday found Papa making preparations for a trip to town. As he hitched old Blarney to the wagon, he made sure an ample supply of gunny sacks lay beneath the seat. He would need them when he stopped by Grandpa Simms's house to deliver the things he'd purchased for him in town.

And then there were the Benders, the Lennons, the Greens, and Uncle Pettigrew. With his indelible pencil Papa wrote their lists also in his little brown book and delivered their supplies to their doorsteps without fail.

All without pay, of course. But he didn't expect wages in going the second mile for his neighbors. That was part of his belief in the Savior's teachings.

A frosty morning in mid-November was not a "town Saturday," however. It was a Saturday between the trips to town, a "mill day," we called it.

As he loaded up the sacks of corn we'd shelled the previous night, Papa called to Mama, "I may be late, Betsey. I'll have to wait for all the sacks to be ground, you know."

The other sacks of corn to be ground into meal included those belonging to the same families for whom he'd shopped the week before. Papa didn't mind doing it, however. After all, Grandpa Simms was old; Lorena Bender needed help if anyone did; Charlie Lennon had pleurisy; and the Green spinsters had no close kin to do for them.

No, Papa didn't mind the way his Saturdays were consumed for other people. Except, perhaps, for one person. He spoke of him this morning.

"Pettigrew could help me out sometimes if he would," he observed quietly, as he checked Blarney's harness. "Instead of whittling around all day."

"I know," agreed Mama with alacrity, happy that Papa had at last awakened to the fact that his younger brother imposed incessantly on him.

"I've helped him all these years," said Papa slowly, remembrance spacing his words.

"That's just the trouble, Will. You've helped him too much," answered Mama tartly. "He leans on you instead of standing alone."

"If only he'd exert a little more get-up-and-go," sighed Papa.

"Too lazy to take his own corn to the mill," Mama commented acidly, speaking her mind for once about Uncle Pettigrew. "I'll bet he's still in bed. And it already going on eight o'clock!"

"He's my special cross," said Papa in a low tone, sighing once more as he left.

I thought about this after he drove away. All that day

I remembered the term Papa used for his younger brother.

"Everyone has crosses of one sort or another to bear," Mama reflected that afternoon. As I set a plate for Papa, I knew what his cross was—Uncle Pettigrew!

That evening as the sun crept closer to the rim of the hill, the wind dipped up and down in little breezes that almost whistled among the fodder shocks. Papa was so late getting back that we became unduly concerned. John and Jim did the milking. Jerry fed the rest of the stock. Then he and I carried in the coal and kindling. Darkness had surrounded Deep Valley when we finally heard the wagon by the gate.

Quickly the boys ran out to unhitch Blarney and carry in the meal. When they returned they were leading Papa —and Uncle Pettigrew! Both were black and sooty. Papa's hands were badly scorched and Uncle Pettigrew's right arm was burned.

"What happened?" cried Mama, running to Papa.

"Pettigrew's house burned," he answered slowly.

"If Will hadn't stopped with my meal I'd never have got out in time," said Uncle Pettigrew. "I was asleep, I guess," he finished lamely.

I looked up at Uncle Pettigrew, remembering he was Papa's special cross. But he didn't look like a cross, not like the ones in the Sunday school papers. To me he was just Uncle Pettigrew, who liked to whittle leisurely with his knife, who wasn't too fond of people, and who preferred living by himself. Unlike Papa, he didn't like to work at all. And he would never go the second mile for anyone. It would be too much trouble for him.

After that, Uncle Pettigrew lived with us. He helped with the chores, read to Timmy and me, and started going to church, something he'd never done previously. In a few months he accepted Christ as his Savior—and that made all the difference.

From that hour Uncle Pettigrew became a changed person, a new man. He shed his old habits of indolence as locusts shed their useless skins. Soon he began working in the mines. Then Saturdays he started going the second mile—and the third and fourth—with Papa, helping the folks who needed aid with their groceries, notions, and loads of corn. When Papa started a Boy's Club in Grandfather Jennings's old barn the next spring, Uncle Pettigrew helped there, too. He directed the boys in their carving and leather work projects.

"Everyone has crosses of one sort or another to bear," Mama observed on a sunlit day in early May as she started to houseclean.

"But God helps us to bear them as they arise," Papa replied. "Sometimes He turns them into blessings. Special blessings," he added thoughtfully, looking at his younger brother.

"Betsey, will this be all right now?" asked Uncle Pettigrew, holding up the latest wall plate he had carved.

"Oh, Pettigrew!" exclaimed Mama, smiling gratefully at him. "That will be perfect for the mantel."

I looked at Uncle Pettigrew. His shoulders were erect as he held the lovely plate.

Why, he was no longer Papa's "special cross." Instead, he had become a special blessing. And all because Papa believed in going the second mile.

# 9

# Someone Knocking at the Door

After Uncle Pettigrew stopped being Papa's cross he grew acquainted with God and himself. Prayer and soul searching led him to carve his own unique notch in the community.

"All human longings seek a matching fulfillment," Papa reflected. "How wonderful that Pettigrew's now flow in the right channel."

Uncle Pettigrew quit the mines and started working in Milton Tanner's woodworking shop. The next week Mr. Tanner invited him to bring his bed down to the little attic room over the shop. Mama gave my uncle a feather bed and several household items and he set up bachelor headquarters at the shop.

A few months later Mama visited Grandma Simms. She returned to disclose the latest news.

"Will," she began thoughtfully, as she pushed the darning thread through her needle, "Pettigrew is making plans to build a new house. And for a very good reason indeed."

She waited for Papa to display a shred of interest in his brother's plans. But absorbed in the almanac, he made no reply. Darning the hole in his sock, Mama pushed her needle through determinedly. With determination, too, she continued the conversation.

"Will, did you know that Pettigrew is courting Eliza Green?"

Papa gazed out the window to observe the pale January sun. He turned and stared directly at his left shoe.

"Will Jennings!" Mama's blue eyes flashed fire. "You knew it all the time, and here I have had to learn the doings of my own in-laws from other people!"

"Well," Papa admitted, concentrating on his shoe as if it were his first lesson in confronting footwear, "I did hear a fraction of the event in the store yesterday."

"Yesterday!" exploded Mama. "And you've hoarded the news for 23 whole hours! Why, Will, I always divide choice morsels of events with you."

Buttoning her lips tightly, Mama with an impetuous gesture laid her mending aside. She rose to check the milk for churning. Not until she'd churned and was beating the butter energetically, did she deign to speak to Papa again. The sentences she squeezed from him then revealed that he was more than a little concerned about his brother's contemplating marriage so late in life. Pettigrew was stubborn and mightily set in his ways, Papa said.

Be that as it may, however, Uncle Pettigrew was actually growing interested, it appeared, in gentle, industrious little Eliza Green. And as Mama disclosed, too (Papa had not known this morsel of news to hoard for himself), Hermann Kiser had started courting her elder sister. Wholly unlike small, meek Eliza, Martha, tall and spare of frame, knew precisely how she desired things done.

"And a will to see that the schedule is run to the hour she sets the clock," Mama commented. "Well, I can say this, if Eliza takes Pettigrew, she can be mistress in her kitchen for once."

"Perhaps," replied Papa briefly.

"And if Hermann and Martha team up, those motherless children will have someone to look after them. I'm sure Martha will be good to them, despite her domineering methods and rather fractious behavior."

"Now, Betsey," reproved Papa.

"Will, I didn't mean . . ." Mama began. "Oh, you men," she muttered, "You never understand!"

The days passed quickly with unfolding episodes. Aunt Noreen's triplets took the chicken pox. And Longfellow, Charlie Lennon's big brown bay, became ill with the lampas. As they recalled how they relied on Longfellow's service for spring plowing, the neighbors vied with each other in dropping free advice on experimental cures.

While everyone stayed busy checking on the bay's recovery Uncle Ralph and Aunt Sarah Hathorne sold their farm down the river and bought Sam Lightner's place, which had now sold twice since Sam moved. It was good to have the two old people for neighbors along with their nephew, Jack Elkins. Both Mama and Papa liked the crusty, cantankerous 73-year-old Ralph Hathorne despite his abominable manners.

Spring hovered on the threshold before stepping tentatively into our valley. Papa planted his spring crops. The hoeing came then and summer unloaded an avalanche of labor. Yet even with the work hemming in, Papa made time for the Bible studies in our home and for the Boys' Club in Grandfather's old barn.

Pastor Horne began helping him there. Uncle Bartley came with Laddie, his adopted son, and lent a hand with the debates. And hard as it was to believe, Uncle Pettigrew joined the group when he wasn't working or passing the time of day with Eliza. Even Hermann Kiser, bringing little Tony, dropped in occasionally. He didn't join in the activities, though. Instead, he sat in the corner and read Grandfather's books on astronomy.

Laddie and Jack Elkins were good debaters, but neither could compete with the speaking abilities of Paul Trainer, Clayton, and Stephen. Especially Stephen. For at long last, despite my love for Clayton, I knew that Stephen Malone was the most talented speaker of all. My friend, Janetta Lane, rooted for Paul while Mama and Papa, of course, felt that Clayton debated supremely.

Clayton was chosen to compile the topics for future debates. In a moment of exhilaration he chose the subject, "Are Women More Curious than Men?" for the next debate.

Hearing of the topic (from Grandma Simms rather than Clayton), Mama managed to withhold her opinion three whole days. By that time she was simply bursting with words.

"This matter of curiosity!" she exclaimed on a hot July evening, as we sat stringing beans on the back porch. "Why, it takes no special discernment to see how all of you will line up against Jenny and me."

Mama defended her sex by asserting that the curiosity of herself and her friends ran in a natural, wholesome channel. It couldn't be classed as prying in the sense that menfolk sometimes inferred was the case. A healthy curiosity merely proved one to be interested in the life threads woven daily around marriage, births, deaths, and varied human relationships built from the necessary processes.

Only through a healthy curiosity could one sense delight in observing the God-given roles people played in the community, Mama declared. One sensed awareness that others, too, were involved in the total living that went with harvesting crops, preparing meals, and the creation of walls, floors, and possessions into a home. The natural, human curiosity connected with these, Mama said, raising her left eyebrow in thought, made life meaningful for her.

"Actually, Will, you're interested also in these. Still, if we women do talk more about people and their doings," she admitted rather grudgingly, "why, I say that's exactly as God intended. After all, they're His most important creation."

"Betsey, you're going around in circles. It's a good thing you're not on the debating team."

"Well, if I were I'd certainly dish out a slice of my belief! I'd declare first of all that the title of that debate is worded wrong. Another thing, I don't like the implications the boys plan to use."

"Implications, Mama? Who's using implications?" Clayton asked in his teasing manner.

Mama, however, intent on such a serious issue, wasn't to be turned lightly from her stirred up feelings. Rather, my brother's attempt to introduce gaiety nettled her all the more. For ever since Papa had reproved her for speaking of Martha Green's dominating manner, she'd felt condemned. And that wasn't a mere isolated case either. There had been other occasions lately when she'd merely felt like "discussing" the neighbors' lives with him and he'd "inferred," so she said now, that she indulged in gossip.

Most of all, though, she hadn't forgotten that he'd known of his brother's courtship 23 whole hours and hadn't confided in her.

"Yes, when we women mention people, we gossip!" Mama concluded her piled up grievances. "But when you men do . . ."

For once in her life then, she grew too vexed for words.

We were surprised to see our usually placid Mama in such a vehement state.

While she continued to snap beans vigorously, Papa ignored her thread of thought to dwell on the curiosity of his own sex. Many famous men, he said, had left priceless contributions for posterity, because of an inquiring nature.

"Now there's Pasteur, who searched for germs," he began. "And Edison's inventions. And David also, who probed into almost every vibration of the human heart. All these, through curiosity, produced wonders for mankind."

Despite Papa's mention of David, her favorite poet, his last sentence did nothing to placate Mama. Rather, it made her feel he was "inferring" that men through curiosity made valuable contributions, whereas women . . . But she already knew how the masculine population displayed a narrow doctrine there.

Clayton evidently sensed a slight apprehension on the debate. "Stephen," he said, "this subject centers around more than we bargained for!"

After that Mama remained silent and hurt for 49 hours and 20 minutes.

On Thursday we went to bed early. Our devotional hour for two nights now had been strained to an uncomfortable degree because the prayers our parents uttered didn't seem natural somehow. Instead, they now prayed in a cool, formal manner. The atmosphere was stale like four-day-old cornbread forgotten in the cupboard. God didn't seem near at all amid such formalism. He seemed as far away as Venus, Grandfather's evening star.

That night a thunderstorm awakened us. In the darkness between the lightning streaks someone knocked on our door. In terrified panic Mama turned to throw her arm around Papa's huge, comforting form. (For two nights now she'd slept on the far side of the bed with her back to his in a frigid, unbending manner.)

"Will, someone's knocking at the door!"

"Betsey," said Papa tenderly, as he enfolded her tiny, frightened figure in his stalwart arms. The moment of forgiveness had arrived, a moment too meaningful for words.

There wasn't time for conversation. Rising hurriedly, Papa ran to open the door. On the threshold stood old, cantankerous Ralph Hathorne, dripping puddles from his wrinkled coat.

"Will," he stammered, his shoulders drooping pathetically, "I got scared out there in your barn. You see, I've slept there for—two nights now."

"You've slept in our barn!" exclaimed Mama, who now stood by Papa. "But come in, Uncle Ralph. I'll hunt dry clothes for you."

Clayton and Stephen soon had a fire burning in the fireplace which dispelled the dampness and chill of the house. As we sat near the bright flames, Uncle Ralph drank Mama's hot cocoa. He gulped it as if he hadn't tasted anything hot for days.

"I hate to tell our family squabbles," the old man confided at last. "But you see, trouble's been brewing between Sarah and me a considerable spell."

As he helped Mama prepare more cocoa, Clayton couldn't refrain from grinning impishly.

"Now, Son," she said, as she smiled lovingly at her firstborn in the manner that was really Mama. When she reached Papa a cup, she gave him a smile that spilled the love and contrition of her heart.

"No, Sarah and me just can't see things along the same eye level," sighed Uncle Ralph. "That is, not since coming to Deep Valley."

"What's the valley got to do with your trouble?" asked Mama without thinking.

The boys and I smiled, remembering how she so often reprimanded us for inquisitive questions. Close by her side, Papa didn't so much as blink an eye at her curiosity since he also itched to hear the answer.

"Well, it's like this." The old man sipped his cocoa more slowly. "Down the river we lived near a church and Sarah attended it. I didn't go, since I don't hold with no church, even if they're located right at heaven's door. Yet I never hindered her from going."

He stopped to wipe his black-rimmed spectacles.

"After we moved here it was a sore point with Sarah to miss her meetings. She won't attend your Presbyterian church. Says she can't hitch up with such newfangled methods. It's the old Baptist doctrine she's hankering to hear, and it's no closer than Lonesome Cove. She's mad 'cause I won't take her over the mountain. Seems to me she could attend church here. We had a row Tuesday night and I left home."

Again Clayton smiled teasingly at Mama. Tuesday was the night she exploded.

The next morning the creek flowed hurriedly by in coffee-colored waves. About 10 o'clock Jacob Trelawney came running up to our gate.

"I've hunted all over for you, Mr. Hathorne. Your nephew Jack has been hurt in the mine!"

Uncle Ralph was so flustered he almost dropped his spectacles. "I shouldn't have urged the boy to earn his keep," he mourned. "At 17 he's too young for the mines." Tears squeezed from his pale blue eyes, dripping on his leathery, old cheeks. He couldn't wait to reach the hospital.

However, Jack wasn't hurt seriously. On learning the

glad news, Mr. Hathorne rushed home to tell Aunt Sarah and make his peace with her.

That afternoon Clayton studied the blue sky as if he were enrolling in an astronomy course. "There's nothing like a heavy thunderstorm to clear the air," he observed sagely. "And all the fear stemming from it," he added as an afterthought.

Papa for once ignored his oldest son. He turned to Mama and spoke directly to her.

"How marvelous that God still loves us even when we fail in love for each other and Him. There is nothing like the misunderstandings of others to bring two people who love each other closer together," he told her, sending love darts from his brown eyes straightway to hers. Ignoring the rest of us, he seemed not to care a whit that he had an audience.

"Oh, Will," said Mama fondly, not caring either as she reached up to ruffle his dark hair.

That night in our devotional hour, Papa and Mama prayed from their hearts for forgiveness and more consecrated love. And the atmosphere was as clear as the fresh spring water where Mama kept her wooden butter molds, with God's presence once more there among us, rather than far away on Venus.

The boys never did debate the subject on the curiosity of the sexes. Too many interpretations of the word kept popping up, Clayton decided.

Soon after Jack's accident, Uncle Ralph began taking Aunt Sarah over the mountain to the Baptist church. He stood around outside, waiting for the service to end. As for Jack, he went to church with us. Frequently we passed Uncle Ralph and Aunt Sarah on their way to the church she preferred. We waved and sent greetings to our friends in Lonesome Cove.

The next summer Stephen and Timmy went to Ohio

to stay with their uncle. It was hard to sit down at the table and observe their two empty seats. In the autumn when the three older boys started to high school, leaving only Jerry and me with our parents, the vacant places accumulating with the years spread to all corners of the house.

The holidays, though, helped chase the emptiness away. Again the boys rushed in, bringing cheer and hilarity. We couldn't wait for the trio to arrive—Clayton with his affectionate, teasing mood, John wrapped in his thoughts, and smiling shyly, and Jim bouncing everywhere in his dramatic manner.

It was during the Thanksgiving holiday that Mama and Papa ran into another disagreement. Mama wanted a new kitchen rug; Papa felt the barn needed a roof more.

Clayton laughed suddenly. "Someone's knocking at the door!" he cried in realistic terror, pretending feminine panic.

"Oh, Clayton," said Mama, ruffling his dark hair, so much like Papa's.

"Oh, Will," she said gently then, reaching for Papa's arm. "The blessings that are ours."

"Betsey," said Papa, brushing his tall son aside to hold Mama close, "marriage is the most sacred institution next to the church."

In that moment I don't think he really saw Clayton or anyone else. He just saw Mama.

# 10

# The Givingest Church Member

On the last Sunday in October Uncle Pettigrew married Eliza Green, and Hermann Kiser stood as the bridegroom of her sister Martha.

"Such a lovely wedding," sighed Mama, when we left the church. "Oh, Will, I always cry at weddings. What will we do when our boys walk down the aisle?"

She looked at Papa and he spoke of Clayton and John, who had left for college in September, and Jim and Jerry, now both in high school.

"Life doesn't unroll in static chapters," Papa said.

He looked at me. "Little Sister may leave us someday, too," he mused, as he smoothed my hair, which I now wore flowing on my shoulders rather than in tight pigtails.

"Oh, no!" cried Mama. "I hadn't even considered Jenny's leaving us."

Papa's brown eyes rested thoughtfully on me. "Little Sister is nearly 12 years old, Betsey."

"Um," said Mama, as she stepped into our buggy.

"Will," she began, arranging her sky-blue shawl around her shoulders, "Eliza's eyes shone like Easter dawn today when she spoke of the new house Pettigrew has built."

"If only my brother will halfway cooperate with her," sighed Papa. "I can't forget how he expected Mother to wait on him when he was the only one left at home. Of course he has changed greatly since he joined the church."

"Yes," affirmed Mama. "With God steering one's course, the heart and eyes see more clearly."

Papa remained silent so Mama continued. "Eliza and Pettigrew will do all right, I think. It's Martha and Hermann that worry me. She still takes those moody spells, I hear, when she imagines herself again standing alone over her mother's deathbed. Why, sometimes she remains depressed and irritable for days. And of course," Mama added, forgetting she'd covered this ground previously, "Hermann will have to toe the mark with her."

"Now, Betsey," reproved Papa mildly. "Let's just tend to our own marriage, with God's help, and let well enough alone."

So Mama and Papa did just that, except that in the next week or so Mama made more trips than usual to visit Grandma Simms. Naturally, she couldn't be blamed for listening to news which was exactly opposite from what both she and Papa had waited to hear.

To her amazement she learned that Eliza, after being ruled by her older sister, was exerting her will and seeing that Uncle Pettigrew shaved every day and said grace at the table. In addition to these reforms, he now cleaned his shoes at the threshold and mopped floors for Eliza.

"And only the Lord and the two of them know what else," said Grandma, undoubtedly aching to be in on the trio. "Marriage has cured Pettigrew of his bachelor, pettish ways, and no one can accuse Eliza of being meek these days."

As for the Hermann and Martha compact, Hermann had scared Martha into obedience the first time she took a moody spell. He'd better never hear of her acting that way before his children again, he said. Everybody held rein over some corner of fear inside, he told her, since it was the price one paid for remaining sane.

After that Martha never again grew upset over past memories. She proved to be a model stepmother and waited hand and foot on Hermann, even cleaning his shoes for him.

"Which just goes to show," Mama summed up the developments, "that situations change constantly, and human nature most of all."

"Nothing is as permanent as change itself," Papa replied sagely.

Since he was relieved about Uncle Pettigrew, Papa lost no time in turning to another problem. That afternoon he and Pastor Horne discussed our population growth.

Shelton Town, the county seat, was growing daily and many town residents had moved out to our valley. Also, with the young generation marrying fast, several new, modern houses now altered our landscape.

"The Sunday school enrollment soared again yesterday," Pastor Horne said.

"We need to expand with more Sunday school rooms," Papa replied.

The two decided on three additional rooms, and the next Sunday the pastor placed the matter squarely before the church.

"We can't turn children hungry to hear God's Word away from His house," he proclaimed earnestly. "Everyone must sacrifice, of course, if we build the rooms."

Milton Tanner spoke right up in church. "Reckon if

we can't sacrifice for the Lord's business, we'd better re-examine our values," he said. Milton hadn't wavered an instant in furthering the Christian gospel since the snowy night when he'd been converted in a fodder shock.

Aunt Eliza nudged Uncle Pettigrew, and he rose to his feet.

"Milton and I will make the tables and chairs for the rooms, won't we, Milt?"

"We women will plan a sewing sale and buy the windows," Aunt Eliza offered.

"And don't forget the doors and nails," Martha Kiser reminded her sister across the aisle. "And what about the lumber itself?"

"I'll make the curtains," decided Magdalene Lane.

Suggestions came right and left all over the room. That was the way we carried on church business in those days—right on Sunday morning directly after the sermon, when everyone was present and in a favorable mood to act on Pastor Horne's prodding us to necessary Christian service. As we spoke informally there in God's house about His business, we felt the Lord was present, too.

On Monday morning the men started preparations for building. For three days the labor proceeded as if nothing else mattered. But on Thursday we learned that something other than labor came first.

At two o'clock that morning Uncle Ralph Hathorne knocked frantically on our door. And this time he had *not* slept in our barn. He'd been sleeping soundly by Aunt Sarah when he awoke to find she'd died in her sleep.

He sat pathetically in our kitchen twiddling his gnarled old fingers, taking off his spectacles, and putting them on repeatedly. The last trace of his contrariness and cantankerous spirit vanished as he confided the dream he'd dreamed that night.

"The dream waked me up," he moaned brokenly. "In

the dream I stood on a mossy creek bank near a waterfall. It was the greenest, most fertile valley I ever saw. And—Sarah stood at the top of the water above me. I tried to climb up to her but she motioned for me to remain where I was. She pointed to a beautiful knoll on the hill opposite me. 'See the church there, Ralph,' she said. She said it over and over.

"But I couldn't see any church. I walked right up to the mountain but still couldn't see a church. It was the most real-to-life dream I ever had."

Aunt Sarah's funeral was held Sunday morning. That afternoon we attended another funeral, that of Millie Bollen and her twins. She died in giving birth to them, and they were stillborn. Lem Bollen, like Uncle Ralph, was almost beside himself with grief.

Late Sunday evening Mama spoke of the four deaths in awe.

Papa sat watching the thin pencil rays trickling from the November sun. "Confucius had something to say about occasions like this," he said, recalling a quote from a favorite author.

"The great mountain must crumble," he quoted. "The strong beam must break, and the wise men wither away like a plant."

Mama looked around the room. "This change is something to consider a mite," she murmured quietly. "The boys' departure, the marriages, births, and deaths . . ."

"But God is back of all physical environment and the invisible one screened from our view. The withering process is not the end of the story." Papa was remembering his Christian faith. "Surely in His orderly universe God doesn't extinguish lives like mere candle flames. The most meaningful object He has created—man's soul—is too intricately woven for the limitations of earth. That's why a larger world, where we can develop further spiritually, awaits our graduation."

"Our graduation," echoed Mama softly, as she savored the words.

"Why, yes," Papa answered positively. "We merely graduate to a higher level of experience when the scissors of death cuts the life thread binding us to earth."

"Oh, Will." Mama's eyes grew tender. "You have such a perfect knack of getting to the core of thought. A lot more accurately than Confucius, I think."

The next week labor on the Sunday school rooms again failed to unfold. A heavy snowfall showered down and the snow held on for weeks.

"We should have known," Papa admitted. "The same circumstance occured when we built the church."

"It's just that you and Pastor Horne are such go-getters, Will," smiled Mama. "Once you get an idea in your head, you want to hurry the steps along."

"Steps?" echoed Papa. He reached for his hat. "Betsey, I promised to visit Uncle Ralph today."

Papa must have witnessed well that day. And the next afternoon Pastor Horne surely succeeded in witnessing effectively also—because at the close of the service on Sunday morning Uncle Ralph walked down the aisle and knelt at the altar. It was such a heartwarming event that one intuitively sensed a good feeling inside toward everyone else who was there, Papa said. That was the highlight of conversions, Mama replied, the fact that they united people in renewed love and Christian fellowship.

"Reckon I've needed God to help me ever since Sarah and me lost our little boy years ago, the only child we ever had," Uncle Ralph spoke brokenly. "But instead of turning to Him I just let my grief set me contrary in my ways. Acting so ornery and not even considering her feelings, I was never good enough to . . . Sarah. And you too, Jack."

He turned to his nephew. "I've been cross-grained with you also. But it'll be different now, boy."

Again we were experiencing a glorious informality in church, as we often did with conversions.

Papa had once read that Presbyterians were sometimes judged to be cool and reserved. "Such can't be said of us, though," he'd observed at the time. "Sometimes we feel as good as the shouting Methodists or the happy Baptists."

"And just what's wrong with shouting and being happy?" Mama had answered heartily. "Especially when one senses gratitude to his Lord."

Beside the altar now, Uncle Ralph expressed his gratitude. "I've built up my land and prospered despite hard times. With the Lord's help, that is, except that I've been too stubbornish to realize the truth."

He took off his black-rimmed spectacles, examining them in a deliberate manner.

"Hear you're building new rooms for the young ones," he spoke slowly. "Now I want to do my share in that blueprint. But above all . . ."

He put on his spectacles, then took them off again. "I'm giving what's left of this old body to the Lord. Too bad I almost let it wear out before offering its service."

We built the Sunday school rooms in the spring. Every member of the church contributed something to further the gospel. Yet no one gave more than Uncle Ralph Hathorne. He threw in money with each new load of lumber and paid completely for a fourth Sunday school room in memory of his little boy.

His giving to the church, of course, had much to do with the neighbors' bestowing on him the title of "the givingest church member."

"But deep down, I believe, they remember something else, too," Papa discerned. "I doubt if anyone will ever forget the Sunday that Uncle Ralph gave the most valuable gift—himself—to Jesus."

"This giving has changed us all," reflected Mama. "We've grown up an inch or so in our sacrifice."

"Events affect people differently." Papa lifted his right hand to his chin in thought. "Now take Uncle Ralph. His sorrow has brought him to God's throne of grace. But as for Lem Bollen . . ."

Mama stared out the window. "Lem is drowning his troubles in drink, just as he always did."

Papa studied his left shoe. "I've tried to talk to Lem, yet failed to help him know God's plan of salvation." He sighed deeply.

"Death and tragedy are not the worst that can happen to one," Papa deliberated in dropping pebbles of thought, "since character growth can increase mightily from the two. The lowest thing that can engulf any man is to deny God and view life as meaningless while standing apart from the love of others."

"Lem loved Millie so," mused Mama slowly. "I keep thinking of the changes—so many in the valley now."

"Death is the final change," reflected Papa. "Uncle Ralph agreed with me today that it is only a continuation of life, though, the supreme paragraph."

"Will," exclaimed Mama then, and she couldn't help laughing softly, "just think how pleased Aunt Sarah must be as the wife of the givingest church member! I don't think it matters at all to her that Uncle Ralph joined our church, instead of the one she preferred. Don't you agree, Will?"

Papa smiled a rare smile and then watched the May sunlight on the windowpane.

# 11

# Papa's Only Shirt

"I'll iron your papa's shirts today," said Mama on Thursday morning. She'd made that particular statement every Thursday since I could remember.

She meant Papa's white shirts, of course—the ones he wore to church and school. On Thursdays he wore a light blue shirt to school. In the evenings and on weekends he worked on the farm in two faded flannel shirts.

I often envied Mama the important task of ironing Papa's white shirts. She allowed me to iron the light blue shirt sometimes. But I was never permitted to iron the white shirts. Mama reserved that vital labor for herself.

"Someday . . ." she said, her voice trailing into an indefinite time. I longed for the "today" one could count upon.

On that particular Thursday, however, a rain-drenched, cloudy morning, Mama did not iron the shirts.

"Someone's stolen your papa's shirts right off the line!" she called back desperately from the porch.

The mines in our region had shut down, and several thefts had been reported lately. Some people had had beans picked out of their fields, potatoes dug, and chickens taken from the hen houses. But clothes off your clothesline on the back porch! And Papa's white shirts at that!

When he came from school and learned of his loss, Papa didn't speak at first. Instead, a hurt, deprived look rose quietly in his brown eyes, like fog rising doubtfully in early dawn. It reminded me of the little sparrow we'd watched when she found one of her baby birds missing.

Papa spoke at last. "I'll just have to wear this light blue shirt to school every day now. It'll be trouble for you, though, Betsey, having to wash and iron it at night."

"Will, we'll save on something," declared Mama. "You must have your white shirts."

But then a puckered little frown appeared above her blue eyes. I knew she was thinking how it took every penny Papa made in teaching and selling produce from the farm to see us through and keep my four brothers in college. I wished I had loads of money to buy Papa all the white shirts he wanted.

Two days later, when he went to feed the stock, he found Lem Bollen out in our barn, sleeping off his weekly drunkenness.

Everyone in Deep Valley knew that Lem got drunk each Friday night. Now, however, through the interest of Papa and the pastor in his salvation, Lem sobered up enough to attend meeting on Sunday. About once a month he'd get up at the end of the service and confess his sin, then promise to reform. But always, by the next week he'd be dead drunk again.

When Papa brought Lem into the house he was wearing an old overcoat. He kept it on even while eating breakfast because he wore no shirt underneath.

"Not a shirt to my name," he declared, as he reached

for one of Mama's hot biscuits. "Someone must've got it off me while—" his voice dangled the last words as though he couldn't admit what should be said. In confusion he stared at the coffee stain he'd dropped on the tablecloth.

"Someone stole Will's shirts right off the line," said Mama then, her words rather spicy, "though that's not as close, I'd say, as one's own back."

Lem hastily ate the last bite of his biscuit and reached hungrily for another.

"Lem," said Papa thoughtfully, "Bartley would take you on at the store, I believe, if you'd only lay off drink."

"Guess I've got to do something," said Lem, "with not a shirt to my name." His eyes strayed downward to the bacon and gravy on his plate.

"I'll try to get you the job," continued Papa. "But you can't let me down. You'd be my responsibility, you know."

"You'd really help me like that?" asked Lem slowly. "After the way I've been all these years."

"You quit once, you know," Papa reminded him.

"Yes, when Millie first took sick," reflected Lem quietly. "I stayed off drink five months. But when she and the twins died after we'd waited years for children—" Tears came to his eyes.

"You can do it again," said Papa firmly. "With a will of your own and the help of the Lord."

"You'll really help me like this, Will?" asked Lem Bollen again in wonderment.

"Betsey," said Papa, looking at Mama in staunch determination, "hunt up my red flannel shirt for Lem to work in. And he and I will take turns wearing my light blue one to church."

Mama started to interrupt, but Papa ended decisively, "It isn't seemly for a man to visit his Lord's house every

Sunday in a flannel shirt. Lem and I will take turns wearing the blue shirt to church."

"But, Will," said Mama.

"Betsey," said Papa. Her eyes fell tenderly on him then, all filled with love and trust, yet somehow mixed with hopelessness and doubt.

The next day Papa persuaded Uncle Bartley to take Lem on at the store. As the weeks passed Lem continued steadily at his job, even on Fridays and Saturdays. Apparently he had, at last, forsaken the evils of alcohol and was doing good work, Uncle Bartley said.

At home, Mama and I weren't thinking of Lem Bollen's job, however, We thought instead of Papa's only decent shirt.

"His only shirt," Mama would say when she'd start ironing. "I'll iron your papa's only shirt today. His only shirt," she'd repeat. "And he has to share it with Lem Bollen."

Not telling Papa, she wrote the boys about his loss. Clayton and John, Jim and Jerry had answered that they were working extra to buy Papa a white shirt for Father's Day. Mama was saving from the egg money. Since I helped with the hens, the shirt she'd buy would be a present from both of us, she said.

On Father's Day, Mama, the boys, and I proudly laid our gifts beside Papa's plate. He opened his presents and found five new shirts. His brown eyes filled with love and thankfulness.

Eating and talking away, we barely heard the light knock on the door. "For you, Will," said Lem Bollen, as he reached a large bundle to Papa.

When Papa opened the package he found five new white shirts!

"Will," said Lem in a halting manner, "they're not a present, really. They're yours by rights. You see," he stopped, then held his shoulders upright as if to grasp new courage.

"You see," he began again, "I took your shirts off the line and sold them for drink over in Lonesome Cove. I sold the shirt off my back, too," he admitted, his voice low.

For several moments no one said a word. Papa broke the silence at last.

"Why, thank you, Lem," he said. "I consider the shirts a present anyway. Because you've more than repaid me by living up to my belief in you. But it isn't seemly for a man to own 10 new white shirts all for himself."

"It's better than having only one shirt to your name," said Mama tartly, then added tenderly, "You deserve every one of them, Will."

"We'll wear white shirts to church today, boys," said Papa happily in anticipation. "All of us. A man should enter his Lord's house in a white shirt."

Later, in church he turned to Lem, who was wearing a brand new white shirt of his own and standing straight and tall, with not a trace of his drunken limp.

Papa looked, too, at his four tall sons, who had never tasted an alcoholic beverage. Each of them wore a clean white shirt.

"The Lord is good to us," he whispered gratefully to Mama.

That day Lem Bollen made a profession of faith and repentance which didn't have to be renewed each month.

"Ten white shirts to iron," said Mama that afternoon, her eyes resting speculatively on me. "Jenny, can you help me iron the white shirts on Thursday?"

"Oh, Mama!" I said, before running to stand near Papa. Because this was his day—Father's Day. and I was proud of him. He'd shared his only shirt with a man in whom he believed, and the bread he'd cast upon the water had been returned to him tenfold.

# 12

# The Boy Who Became a Methodist Minister

Papa had been having trouble with his heart. But in his happiness over Mr. Bollen's conversion he almost forgot his condition. With new vigor he tended his summer crops and walked with his Bible at eventide in his garden. In the autumn he stood there in silent gratitude. The bountiful harvest would help pay the boys' school expenses.

Although Papa checked carefully on his bank account, the lack of money didn't bother him unduly. With God's help behind him, he stretched his dollars. Money, he knew, should never be a prime interest. That was why he grew concerned over young Paul Trainer, who became fascinated with the dollar. Paul was the son of Ben Trainer, who had married Aunt Noreen, Mama's sister, after Uncle Ed died.

"Ben's worried about Paul," Papa commented one day. "With his high school finished, the boy should start to college. But Paul isn't spending the dollars he's saved on further schooling, he told Ben."

"Paul seems obsessed with money somehow," Mama measured her words. "He sleeps with that leather pouch of his under his pillow, Noreen says, and counts his savings each night before going to bed."

"The boy—" sighed Papa.

"He's saved practically every cent his fingers have touched since coming to live with Ben and Noreen. Why, I'll bet he's hoarded almost enough to pay his own way to school."

"The boy needs an education," said Papa quietly. "He has a bright mind."

As I read near the window, I thought of black-eyed, handsome Paul Trainer, who'd become part of our valley life. I wondered what his life had been like when he lived out West with his mother and the uncle who was sent to the penitentiary for counterfeiting.

Mama spoke of Paul's past history now while Papa stared hard at his left shoe, his brown eyes serious.

"Let's talk of something else, Betsey," he interrupted eventually. "I just don't care to think of that boy's early environment."

I turned a page and remembered the story of Silas Marner that Daddy Lovell had read us one winter. Paul especially had been interested in the story of the old miser and his coins. In memory I could see Paul now, tall and handsome beside the old Ben Franklin stove, his dark eyelashes curling above his thoughtful eyes and firm lips parted in a shy smile. He'd stooped to help me with my arithmetic and his black, wavy hair fell across his forehead.

Paul, like Stephen, had always helped us younger scholars. He was never too busy to help those in need. He'd grown to be a helpful, honest young man with plenty of virtues. Only in the matter of clutching his pocketbook a shade tightly was Paul Trainer lacking.

"Will," said Mama a few days later, "I've learned why Paul isn't going to college. Janetta Lane is back of it all, Noreen says."

Janetta Lane?" said Papa.

"Yes. She has marriage on her mind and everyone knows she's always had her eyes on Paul."

That afternoon in girlish confidence Janetta told me she meant to marry Paul soon. She couldn't wait forever for a wedding ring, she said.

"But a handsome, intelligent boy like Paul is worth waiting for!" I said.

"Oh, Jenny," she replied impetuously, "what do you know about Paul, or any other boy, at your age?"

Beneath her gaze I felt the color rise over my plain face which, despite my studious application of buttermilk and lemon juice, still held 21 freckles. I'd always wear freckles on my tanned face along with my mousey-brown hair and solemn gray green eyes, I knew, whereas Janetta with her golden curls and laughing brown eyes attracted everyone.

Although Paul had added to his savings by the end of the year, he didn't marry Janetta. Instead, he began working on a janitorial job at the First National Bank. Papa had talked to Mr. Atwood, the president, after Paul promised Uncle Ben he'd start to college the next year.

In January Mr. Atwood told Papa that Paul kept the bank so shining clean that the patrons commented daily on its cleanliness. A finer, more upstanding boy never lived, Mr. Atwood averred. He didn't shirk physical work and he had a mind for figures, too.

"I shouldn't wonder but what someday he'll be counting bills behind the window instead of shining the glass," Mr. Atwood predicted.

Papa was so pleased over the news that he just had to share it with Pastor Horne.

"I knew all the time that boy had a good, sound head on him," Papa affirmed. "It was just that I worried a mite there over his concern for money. Reckon I couldn't forget what Ben told me about the lad's mother and his early environment."

Pastor Horne looked out the window a long moment. "Yes, Will, the boy is competent and ambitious. He was among the top workers in the Boys' Club."

The pastor meditated as he watched the snowflakes huddle against the windowpane.

"The boy may be lonely boarding this winter with old Mrs. Kelly," he reflected. "I'll speak to the Methodist pastor in town and ask him to invite Paul to church. The Presbyterian church is without a pastor just now and their services are irregular."

As a result of Pastor Horne's interest, Rev. Daniel Denison invited Paul to church. Mr. Atwood was pleased when Paul started going to church. Although he wasn't a church member, the banker attended services faithfully. One Sunday he would attend the First Baptist Church. The next Sunday he might occupy a pew in the Methodist or Presbyterian church. He believed wholeheartedly in all religious institutions, he said, since they took care of people's souls and made them honest in business. One of his best friends was Rev. Denison, with whom he played checkers and discussed religion and philosophy.

One snowy afternoon when Papa came from town, he told us he'd met Rev. Denison and Mr. Atwood on the street.

"The Reverend says he'll make a pastor out of Paul yet," Papa disclosed. "He thinks the boy has a special leaning toward theology. Paul's been helping him out in the Sunday school."

Mama hung Papa's overcoat up with care. She stirred the fire and tested the soup.

"But Mr. Atwood is just as determined to see that Paul becomes a banker."

"Um." Mama reached Papa his soup. "And what does the boy say? It's his life, you know."

"Paul's never said what he wants to be. In fact, Mr. Atwood has been worried about this. The boy seems to have something weighing him down."

A week later Paul knocked on our door. He wanted to see Papa alone. The two talked in our little lean-to room off the kitchen. After Paul left, Papa sat quietly for several minutes. Then he spoke.

"The boy gave me permission to tell his story," he said. "Two weeks ago he found a $20.00 bill on the street. For about 10 minutes he debated what to do. He considered keeping it, but then finally went to the bank and gave the money to Mr. Atwood. He discovered that Rev. Denison had dropped the bill."

Mama lifted her left eyebrow in thought.

"Of course Paul committed no outward sin," Papa continued. "But the fact that he entertained the idea of keeping the money troubles him greatly. The remorse is literally gnawing away at his conscience."

"Um," said Mama. "I wonder if anyone else ever found money and for the space of 10 minutes considered keeping it. Just how would we feel if everyone knew all our inner thoughts? What would the world be like? Would life run more smoothly with tangled relationships straightened out? Or would chaos result in all the confessions?"

Papa lifted his right hand to his chin in thought. "The situation would be something to wonder about, Betsey."

"What did you tell Paul?" asked Mama.

"I told him to stop by in the morning. In the meantime I'll consider the aspects of his problem"

"And pray, of course," said Mama placidly.

"Why naturally, I wouldn't think of offering advice to a young man without listening for God's directions."

By the next morning Papa must have received the Lord's guidance. When Paul came the two again talked in the little lean-to room. Paul held his shoulders resolutely as he left.

I watched him go. And suddenly a past memory made me sense how he felt inside. He was courageous indeed when he confessed his inner thought, I knew.

"Betsey," said Papa, "the boy is one of those few persons who can't feel completely honest till he's brought everything out in the open. Therefore, I advised him accordingly."

"Well—" said Mama, waiting.

"I told him to go to Rev. Denison first," Papa counted his syllables slowly. "And I advised him to talk to Mr. Atwood also. He won't be satisfied till he's fought this trouble through to the core, leaving no hidden seeds."

"Oh, Will, you always know what action to take—after listening for directions from God, of course."

When the minister and banker heard the confession, they almost had an outright disagreement over Paul Trainer's vocation.

"I could never find another that honest to work in my bank!" Mr. Atwood exclaimed with conviction. "I want him to remain with me always because he's true all the way to the inside."

He looked pointedly at the pastor. "Well, after all, who doesn't sense a dishonest thought now and then?" he demanded defiantly.

The pastor meditated. He spoke then on the same idea that Mama had entertained. "I really wonder what the world would be like if all of us knew each other's thoughts." He sighed as if such knowledge would be too heavy a weight on his shoulders.

"Atwood," he said, "you mustn't keep the boy. With his aptitude for things of the spirit, he simply has to be a minister."

"But he knows so much about the value of money!" the banker expostulated.

A week later Paul told us that he was considering the Methodist ministry. Never again, he asserted, would he value money as he had previously. The dollar's value simply didn't mean as much to him now because he'd begun to realize the worth of other possessions. Possessions like peace of mind, a clean conscience, and the privilege of helping others to know Christ's love.

That fall Paul enrolled in college and became the roommate of my brother John. Both studied preparatory courses for the seminary. At home in Deep Valley we awaited their letters.

Paul also wrote to Mr. Atwood and Rev. Denison. The pastor's cup of gratitude had filled to the brim when he learned of Paul's decision. As for Mr. Atwood, he gradually grew reconciled that Paul would never become a banker.

Paul continued to work in the bank during vacations, though. He also assisted Pastor Denison in the church. When he filled in for the pastor, he delivered a sermon that satisfied even Mr. Atwood, who was inclined to watch for defects in theological discourses.

Paul used the remainder of his savings in the seminary. Since Uncle Ben and Aunt Noreen were having a hard time just then caring for her nine children and their triplets, Rev. Denison and Mr. Atwood stepped in to pay the rest of Paul's expenses. Side by side at graduation, the pastor and the banker watched "their boy" walk down the aisle.

A month later old Mr. Denison died in his sleep. Paul

was chosen to fill his pastorate and soon became one of the most competent pastors in town.

"Why, in addition to a new sermon each Sunday, he manages to squeeze money from the misers and collects more for missionary efforts than any pastor yet," one Methodist asserted with pride.

"Yes," agreed another. "Two things about the young man. He doesn't believe in warmed-over sermons and he certainly has a good business head."

Right away Mr. Atwood began attending the Methodist church regularly. At a Thanksgiving service then, to which churches of other denominations were invited, he went forward at the invitation. Many members of our Presbyterian church in Deep Valley were present, along with people from the town Presbyterian church and the First Baptist. Even some Primitive Baptists from Lonesome Cove attended. Everybody rejoiced over Mr. Atwood's conversion.

"I do declare," exclaimed Mama, shaking hands right and left, "why, here in town it's just like our conversions back home!"

"I've always been for religion," Mr. Atwood declared as he held Paul's hand. "Only now . . ."

He looked around at the group surrounding him—all sincere followers of Christ. There was no need to explain further. Every Christian present knew that he couldn't wait longer to accept the Lord, and that he felt a joyful difference inside now that he had made his commitment to Him. It was a difference that seemed unique to him alone, yet it had been sensed by all in their personal conversions.

Two weeks later Rev. Paul Trainer married Janetta Lane.

Papa's last shred of anxiety concerning Paul vanished completely. "Just what the young man needed—a woman by his side. He's too good-looking to remain an unmarried minister."

However, I held a few reservations on Janetta's ability to be an efficient minister's wife. My fears proved groundless. After having waited for Paul so long, Janetta had acquired patience and understanding. Her outgoing, friendly manner made her a capable, well-liked pastor's wife.

One Sunday I attended the Methodist church with her. Paul built his sermon around the theme that people are more prone to emphasize the point of saving the churches and religion rather than the truth that religion saves us.

"Remember the apostle Paul," the pastor reminded us. "He worked hard to build the church upon Christ's principles. Yet he never failed to relate his own experience on the Damascus road and tell how it changed his own life. He shared this experience, trusting that others might also have a soul examination and learn to know Christ firsthand."

Paul stopped, pushed back a wave of his black hair, and looked squarely at each of us in turn as he drove home his point.

"Such experiences are the core of Christianity," he punctuated each separate word. "They lead us to start with the fragment of faith we possess and trust God for its further growth. A growing faith leads to a mature religion and doesn't need to be defended. Rather, mature religion and faith save us. They lift us to God and, sensing His presence near, we shun the wrong and do the right thing instead."

Janetta turned to smile at me—a significant smile accompanied by the lilt of a question in her eyes. And at that moment I recalled again the memory that had made me understand Paul when he'd considered keeping the money.

On a September morning at the schoolhouse, Janetta and I had admired Paul Trainer's new notebook while he played ball outside. Neither of us had ever owned a sheet of slick notebook paper. We wrote only on rough tablet sheets.

I looked at Janetta; she'd turned to me. Each knew what the other was thinking—"Only one sheet apiece. He'd never know."

But we didn't take the paper. Instead, we had turned slowly and walked out to play with the other pupils.

"Use your religion," Rev. Trainer admonished us, bringing me back to the present. "Used iron does not rust; used muscles do not grow inert. The worst blow one can deal religious faith is to place it on a shelf, reserving it for a rainy day. Today the sun is shining—and people out there need to know God as we know Him. Let's put our faith to work."

I smiled at Janetta Trainer; she smiled at me. Our smiles were of mutual appreciation for her husband's sermon.

# 13

# The New Baptist Church on Pinnacle Mountain

Clayton and John sometimes seemed like twins, since they shared everything. With slightly over a year's difference in their ages they were nearly the same size. Both had thick wavy hair, the darkest shade of brown, which they inherited from Papa. Their eyes—chestnut-colored and velvety—resembled his. John's eyes held the same solemn, studious look as Papa's. Clayton's, though, contained the merry glance of Mama's blue eyes. His happy look bubbled forth in a loving, teasing manner that delighted us all. Yet as the eldest son, he was responsible and helped us younger ones in our decisions.

In his sophomore year at college, Clayton decided to become a teacher of religion at the college level. He'd need more money for another degree, of course, but like Papa, when he scheduled a path of action, my oldest brother permitted nothing to block the necessary steps. In the summers he worked in Mr. Atwood's bank, sold

Bibles and magazine subscriptions, and even worked in the mines.

At college Clayton worked in the cafeteria. He finished college and completed his graduate study, working his way through on his own.

He began teaching in a small Presbyterian college, where he met Beth Shannon, a lovely English teacher. Again my brother wasted no unnecessary time. He and Beth were married after only a few months of steady courtship.

The moment that I laid eyes on my new sister-in-law I knew she was exactly right for Clayton. I watched the two together and contemplated on the mystery that certain people's feelings just naturally flowed in perfect unity.

With a height of five feet and eight inches, Beth stood gracefully by Clayton, who was six feet and three inches, like Papa. She had inherited reddish-blonde hair from a Scotch-Irish ancestry. Her blue violet eyes were shy and gentle.

Quiet and a good listener, Beth took little part in the general conversation. But sitting beside her, one sensed a close companionship. She was one of those rare persons who made you feel at ease without small talk for the sake of politeness.

Mama was delighted with her new daughter-in-law, and Papa also was pleased. Her soft eyes and shining hair reminded him of Grandma Jennings. He enjoyed discussing classical literature and the Bible with her. She had an intelligent mind and a quiet way of probing into worthwhile values.

Yes, all of us loved Beth and vied for her attention. That is, all except John, who had shared so much with Clayton. Now, as he saw Clayton engrossed with his new bride, John felt suddenly lost without an anchor. Since Clayton was so happily in love he didn't notice John's dejected mood, but our parents noted it with concern. They spoke of it after the young couple left.

"Will," said Mama, "John is so different from the other children." A tiny thought-wrinkle pleated her forehead. "Always a loner except for his companionship with Clayton and Paul Trainer. No wonder he's taking it hard that Clayton has broken away from him."

Papa lifted his right hand to his chin in thought.

"I couldn't imagine John interested in a girl!" declared Mama. "He's just so reserved with everyone. His real self seems to live elsewhere in a secret world, and he's been wrapped up in his faith since he was seven."

"I haven't thought of that episode in years," said Papa slowly.

John was barely seven on the December day which changed him from a laughing, fun-loving child to a thoughtful, serious little boy, who appeared older than his years. From that time on he was ever interested in spiritual concepts.

On that December day Papa and Mama had attended service at the old log church on Pinnacle Mountain, taking the two older boys along. Unlike the Sunday on which John was born, the day was mild and fair with a pale blue sky and a gentle wind hopscotching on the windowpanes. John squirmed restlessly. He longed to be playing outside, rather than having to sit still while the preacher exhorted with words beyond his comprehension.

He despaired that the service would ever end. Unexpectedly then, freedom unfolded for him. Right in the middle of Rev. Hasselton's sermon, Howard Tanner's wife began shouting. When she stopped her exclamations of the glory she'd beheld in her emotion, she asked to be baptized immediately.

Everyone prepared to enjoy the welcome event which would be held down at the creek. That is, all but John.

"How he got away from me, I'll never know," Mama wondered now, even after all the years.

"I was walking by Dan Bender," Papa remembered. "He helped us look for John after the others had gone to the baptizing."

"And they came back and helped look, too," Mama recalled gratefully. "We'd never have made it that night if it hadn't been for the neighbors and prayer."

"The night was an unusual experience for a seven-year-old," Papa reflected quietly. "John's never been the same since."

"The event made him what he is today, a boy wrapped in a world of his own thought."

Mama rose to prepare supper. "When John finishes his seminary work he will want to preach, of course. But, Will, just where will he preach? He's never made the slightest impact on any congregation. No church has been interested enough to invite him back."

Papa meditated several moments.

"Betsey, the boy will find himself eventually," he decided. "He has ideas in abundance, of that I'm sure. And if he's truly been called to preach, he'll learn some way to get through to his congregation."

Papa's brown eyes twinkled suddenly. "The perfect solution, perhaps, would be for him to fall in love at first sight, as Clayton did. A spirited woman might just lift the latch to his inner world."

"Um. Well, if such a girl comes along, she'd accomplish what none of us have been able to do!"

That night I thought about John and remembered how some girls at school had tried to push him forward when he couldn't keep up with the games.

My second brother wasn't born with a maimed foot. Only after that night he spent in the cave near the old log church, did he become crippled and change to a premature adult, who sensed thoughts beyond his years.

That sunlit December day when the crowd adjourned for the baptizing, John knew that he'd endured more than enough preaching for one day. He knew someone would preach again down by the creek. Quietly he left the others and slipped over the hill pathway to climb the slope behind the church toward the cave.

From inside the cave he heard voices calling but didn't let on where he was hiding. By now he was enjoying himself mightily as he sensed power over those in search of him. He pushed still further into the cave. Just then a layer of rock came down on his left leg, crushing it and making it impossible to move. Not until nine o'clock the next morning did Papa and Dan Bender find him.

After a few months John could run and play with the help of his crutch, which he never seemed to mind. He didn't pity himself or feel bitter because from then on he walked differently from the rest, limping somewhat even after he laid the crutch aside. That wasn't John's trouble. The injury alone didn't make him different from others.

The difference centered around the imprint of the cave experience, which made him concerned for people in a manner beyond his years. It left him filled with long silences which no one was able to penetrate.

That night he had been frightened, in pain, and alone in the dark. In those agonizing hours he recalled how he'd rebelled against sitting in church, how he'd failed to answer the calls for him, realizing that in so doing he'd brought anxiety to Mama and Papa.

When he fell asleep at last he had dreamed a dream that remained with him always. Only after several months did he relate the memory to our parents. They listened with mixed emotions, unable to believe that a dream could remain such a reality to a child.

"I dreamed about my great-grandfather in the cave," John confided one spring afternoon. "He stood near my right arm and still does sometimes."

"But you never saw Great-grandfather Jennings!" Mama expostulated, her voice climbing in consternation. "You know only what Grandfather has told you about his fiery sermons in the Primitive Baptist church."

"He stood near my arm, Mama," John insisted stubbornly. "And he stands there sometimes now—even in daylight. Of course, I don't really *see* him. But I think he looks like Abraham or Moses. He holds a Bible in his hand and looks like Grandfather, too."

"Nonsense!" said Mama, wholly alarmed by this time. "You've been listening to Grandfather's dreams too much."

"But I do feel Great-grandfather near me sometimes. I really do!"

"Will Jennings!" Ignoring her son, Mama addressed herself to Papa. "Why, oh, why did I ever marry into such an unbelievable family with all their fantastic ideas? Your father and his dreams of the spirit world!"

"Son," began Papa slowly, "now suppose we just talk this out once and for all."

When John saw that Mama and Papa didn't believe him, however, he buttoned his lips and refused to utter another word.

Right after that John started sitting upright in church as if his life depended on erect posture. He begged Papa for more Bible stories and began studying the Bible himself. As he grew older, he read Grandfather's books on spiritualism and his religious history of Josephus. At 12 years he announced that he intended to be a minister.

"I want to be a pastor," he spoke in a rare confidence, "who can make religion simple and real—even for children. A portion of the sermon at least should be directed to them."

Now John had finished college and was almost through seminary. Yet, though in his final year, no pastorate seemed to be opening up.

The Christmas after Clayton's marriage, a special friend of mine in school, the gay, laughing Katrina Brown, went home with me for the holidays. It was love at first sight for her and John. They were married on John's graduation day, and a small church near Clayton's home in Ohio called him to be their preacher.

Mama and Papa were elated that John had ultimately secured a pastorate. They knew of a certainty that things would be different now.

"Of course they will!" Mama declared positively. "Why, John is wholly different since he met Katrina."

Papa's brown eyes twinkled. "What did I tell you, Betsey? Didn't I say that a sprightly woman would pry the boy out of his shell?"

"Yes, she's helped him when we were unable to get through his reticence," Mama commended her new daughter-in-law. "Of course John will always be shy, reserved at times, and ever thoughtful. But now with Katrina by his side, he's more outgoing and speaks all friendly like to everyone, especially to children. I used to think it strange indeed that he planned to preach so they would understand him, and at the same time he rarely noticed any child."

"Well, he really notices them now. Did you see how he made over those youngest ones of Dan Bender's after Katrina held the least one on her lap?"

"That Katrina!" Mama exclaimed delightedly. "She can charm anyone. With that black hair and those Irish, blue green eyes she's as pretty as can be. Yet her attraction, I believe, lies most of all in the sweet and loving nature so natural to her."

"She can talk on any person's level and feels empathy for everyone," said Papa. "That's why she has helped John so much. She is interested in people and is leading the way for him."

Through her charming personality Katrina endeared herself to John's congregation by holding open house at all hours. Never minding household chores undone, she listened to a neighbor's trials, did free baby-sitting, or purchased groceries for those involved in heavy schedules. She cheered the sick and planned clever, useful projects for her Sunday school class and for the invalids.

But above everything, Katrina listened to John's thoughts and helped him convey his ideas effectively in his sermons. Her help and care gave him confidence in himself. He was soon liked by everyone, the young people most of all. In the first year of his pastorate he led 32 young persons, several under 10 years, to accept the Lord.

Perhaps John would have continued on at the little church in the city if unforeseen circumstances hadn't developed, acts of Providence maybe, Papa said later.

On a rainy November day Jack Elkins was killed in the mines after having been hurt in three previous slate falls. John hurriedly rushed home to preach the funeral at Uncle Ralph Hathorne's request.

After the service everyone said John did a marvelous job preaching. But no one liked his sermon better than did Uncle Ralph.

"John," said the old man, who now stalked along in his 80s, "the valley needs you. You owe your talent to your own people rather than to outsiders."

John looked down at the wrinkled old fellow and smiled gently.

"The valley needs you," the old man repeated. "So

I've outlined a plan that may interest you. You see, I dreamed my dream again the night before Jack . . . got killed."

"Your dream!" exclaimed John. He and Katrina looked at each other.

"Yes, the one I've dreamed more than once since Sarah died. In the dream I still see the fertile, green valley and the knoll on the hill where she keeps pointing to a church I've never seen. Now, though, I believe I see the beginning of it."

He looked intently at John, who stood wrapped in thought. Uncle Ralph took off his spectacles and wiped them carefully.

"I know that Sarah didn't mind my joining the Presbyterian church. But still I remember that she preferred the Baptist doctrine. And so—well, you may think I'm woolgathering, putting such stock in dreams. Yet at long last, I see the meaning why she returns to me in that special way."

He spoke positively now, sure of his direction. "Sarah wants me to build a Baptist church. So I'm building a new one on Pinnacle Mountain, where the old log church used to stand."

An incomprehensible look appeared in John's chestnut eyes.

"Of course you're a Missionary Baptist, while Sarah hankered toward the Primitive doctrine," reflected Uncle Ralph. "Still, a peaceful feeling inside tells me that's all right with her. So if I build the church, will you be the pastor, young man? It was only when I heard you preach today that I seemed to receive the final go-ahead for the church."

That night John confided to us that he had never forgotten his own unique dream, which he'd dreamed as a seven-year-old in the cave. He still felt the presence of

Great-grandfather near at times, he said. When Uncle Ralph disclosed his plan, he'd responded inwardly in a very positive manner.

"And always that spot on Pinnacle Mountain has beckoned me," John confided in a low tone. "Today, then —well, the fragments just seem to fit together."

The new Baptist church was built in the spring just above the spot where the old log church had stood. It was a tall, white building with the hillside protecting it and the sky just above, as if heaven were only a stretch or so away. The ancient cave nearby, still dripping moisture, lay within the mountain as a reminder to John that even a seven-year-old can be awakened to spiritual matters.

Each Sunday a large number of young persons attended the new church to hear John preach the gospel story in his simple, direct manner. Many were converted and made their youthful lives count for God.

All 12 of Dan Bender's children became members. One bright September morning, Dan himself walked forward at the invitation. John, in his ministry, at last accomplished what no other preacher had been able to do. Lorena, Dan's wife, had been a Christian long before she died.

Soon after Dan's conversion he became ill and died of pneumonia. John and Katrina, unable to have children, adopted his two youngest boys, nine-year-old Benjie and seven-year-old Tom.

"A family of our own at last! Just think of that, Papa!" Katrina smiled gaily one Sunday as she held the children close.

But John, still thoughtful at times and wrapped in his inner world, didn't answer immediately. Instead, he stared out the window of the church on Pinnacle Mountain toward the cave. More than likely, he was sensing again the presence of Great-grandfather Jennings.

# 14

# The Young Salvation Army Captain

Near the window one December day Mama sat knitting a blue blanket. Papa sat nearby, a new magazine on his knee.

"Beth's baby will come soon," reflected Mama. "I can't wait to see little Clayton."

"Little Clayton, eh?" said Papa.

Busy near the hearth, I labored over charts for student teaching. After graduation I hoped to teach the third grade near Clayton's home.

My parents spoke of Clayton now. He was a successful teacher on the college faculty. His students declared that he made the meaning of the Christian faith plainer than any one had ever done. He was furthering the gospel in his own way, as God intended, Papa declared.

"John, too, is reaching others," Mama said glowingly. "And Jim is doing well in his Methodist church down in Tennessee. Just think," she exclaimed in anticipation, "the boys will be home in two more days! I can't wait to meet Jim's girl friend."

"I wonder if Nora Jane will be as nice as Beth and

Katrina," Papa mused. "Jim says her people are as varied in their religious leanings as we are. In fact, her twin brother is in the Salvation Army."

The next morning, preparations for Christmas became the family's sole concern. Mama hadn't felt well lately and I worked hard to lighten her load. We baked cakes, pies, and cookies; we made mincemeat, meat loaf, and dressing to store in the freezer. Papa and I dressed the chickens and turkey.

By Christmas Eve our homecoming was in full swing. Clayton and Beth arrived first. John, Katrina, and their boys came next. Jerry rode in then, fatigued from his studies in medical school. Stephen and Timmy followed.

Stephen now worked in a business office for his uncle. Like Jerry, he seemed tired that day. But Timmy, a college freshman, was exuberant. After changing his mind repeatedly, our youngest boy had decided to follow Jerry's footsteps and become a doctor.

While Timmy talked to Jerry, I turned to Stephen, noting his withdrawn look. How different he was from the previous Christmas. Then he and I had laughed and talked as we played checkers by the fire.

"Why, Little Sister, you're growing up," he'd said at last. "Where have your freckles gone? I rather liked them, you know."

A tender, thoughtful look had appeared then in his serious, gray eyes and I'd felt the color rising on my face. Stephen had always teased me about my 21 freckles.

Now, a year later, Stephen answered me only briefly, as if his thoughts were elsewhere. Acquainted with his moods through the years, I knew that something was preying on his mind. I wished he could confide in me, but he didn't.

To our disappointment, Jim didn't appear until ten o'clock Christmas morning. He'd been detained by a heavy snowstorm. Nora Jane and her twin brother, Edward, came with him.

The moment Mama laid eyes on the pair, she said she'd have known them to be twins without introductions. Both Nora Jane and Edward were of medium height and had brown, wavy hair. Both had warm brown eyes that sparkled with animation and conviction when they spoke on topics dear to them.

Like Mama, Papa was mightily pleased with his prospective daughter-in-law. He enjoyed meaty and appetizing conversations with her, as he had on first meeting Beth. And he talked and listened intently when he and her brother discussed religious views and their interest in the Salvation Army.

The holiday season passed without dramatic incident, but one concern lingered. It had to do with Stephen's distant mood.

"Betsey," said Papa, "something is bearing on our Stephen's mind."

"*Our* Stephen," Mama echoed fondly. "Yes, he does seem like our own son, doesn't he? But what could be wrong with him?"

Papa lifted his right hand to his chin in his characteristic gesture. "Betsey, that boy isn't cut out to work behind bleak office walls. He's dissatisfied there, I'm sure."

Mama lifted her left eyebrow in thought. "If only we could start him walking in the direction of something challenging and fulfilling—like what Edward Gannon is involved in."

In May, Jim and Nora Jane were married before an altar of flowers in Papa's garden. Edward came, of course, and when he left he promised to write Papa. One evening in a navy-purple twilight, he asked me also to correspond with him.

Two weeks later Papa and Mama, along with the boys and their families, attended my graduation. Timmy and his girl friend sat with our family. Stephen sent word that he couldn't come.

But at the last moment he did come after all. When I received my diploma, I looked for Mama and Papa to convey my gratitude for their making the momentous moment possible. I turned to smile at Stephen. He returned my smile, but back of his serious, gray eyes still lay that sadness that troubled me.

My graduation was the last happy event for several months. Riding into town with John and Katrina the next week, Mama was hurt seriously when their car skidded on a slick highway. She lay in the hospital several weeks, and when she came home she wasn't able to work.

Meanwhile Papa had suffered a heart attack. There was nothing for me to do but to give up my teaching plans and care for my parents. I wouldn't have done otherwise, of course, considering my love and concern. Nevertheless, I wondered about the future.

On a September day of gold sunlight, blue-powdered sky, and a gay breeze, Stephen came home to visit Papa and Mama.

"I kept thinking of you two last night." He looked down from his tall height and his eyes grew tender in solicitous care. "Call it intuition if you like, Mr. Will," he said with a half smile as he ran his sturdy hands through his corn-tassled hair, "but I simply had to come home today."

We sat near the blooming velvet marigolds in the garden—Papa, Mama, Stephen, and I. And the day was the most glorious ever, one that just made you know the world was the loveliest of all places to be, and that, despite everything, problems would unravel to a correct solution.

Perhaps the beauteous day influenced Stephen. At

any rate, he suddenly disclosed that more than one problem troubled him. "Yet I hardly know where to begin."

"Why not start with the first chapter of your distress, Son?" Papa encouraged him.

"The first chapter?" Stephen stared fixedly at the marigolds. "What was the first chapter, I wonder, in the story of the Malone family?"

A wounded look appeared in Stephen's eyes. The look reminded me of the one that had been there years ago when Tim Malone, his father, drowned in Shelton River. Since then I'd often felt that Stephen kept a little corner of sadness reserved inside, even when he appeared to be gay and happy among us.

But Stephen wasn't gay now. In halting sentences he related how his parents had been unhappy together. His words revealed a story wholly unknown to me. Mama and Papa were acquainted with a portion of it, but now Stephen filled in certain details for them. It was a sordid story, almost melodramatic in some places. It was a story of marital confusion compounded with drink.

After he had unloaded his troubled heart into sympathetic and understanding ears there seemed to come over him a great sense of relief.

"I want my life to count in fighting the wrongs of the world," he proclaimed earnestly at last. "I remember how my father died in drunkenness. If only I could find my purpose for life and go after it, as Edward Gannon does."

He looked up at the sky and then turned to look intently at me.

For the first time I didn't return Stephen's look directly. The day before a letter had come from Edward. Between the lines I'd sensed that he was considering me in his dedicated plans. The Salvation Army was a soul-winning organization, and any girl might count herself fortunate to join Edward in his goal.

But it was Stephen Malone who was uppermost in my thoughts the rest of that day. If only he could find his purpose in life, he and the rest of us could get a reprieve from anxiety. And if only he'd stop thinking of me as his little sister maybe I could help. When I made my own life decision I certainly didn't want to be responsible for mixing up the lives of two good men.

The next morning Papa spoke of Tim Malone again. "He was a good man until he started to drink. And Lem Bollen, too. How wonderful, though, that Lem finally gave up the habit and placed his life in the Lord's hands."

I, too, thought again of Lem and Millie and of poor Tim Malone, who'd permitted his life to drift toward the wrong action. I thought of Thena, his wife, unloved and unappreciated. She had labored industriously for the sake of her two sons and done without necessities because her husband squandered his money for drink.

Under sudden impulse and inspiration I decided to write the story in fiction form. It was not my first attempt at putting words to paper but never before had I written under such a sense of inspiration. I built the story around the lovely and pathetic personality of Thena Malone. After carefully revising the manuscript many times, I finally mailed my story to the Salvation Army publication.

Imagine my delight when I received word that the manuscript had been accepted for publication!

"Perhaps I can write after all," I said to Papa.

"I never doubted it for a moment, Jenny," he encouraged me, as always.

A few months later my story was published in *The War Cry*. Edward read it and wrote a letter of enthusiastic congratulations. He wrote something else also in an enthusiastic manner. He asked me to walk through life by his side. I read the letter several times, a catch in my throat as I thought of his young life, dedicated wholly to Jesus Christ.

Nevertheless, after weighing all aspects, I sent a decisive refusal. For in facing the matter squarely at last, I knew that I couldn't marry Edward Gannon, no matter how triumphantly he marched for his faith—because I didn't love him. And the reason I didn't was because I loved someone else instead. Ever since he'd carried my books home from school and helped me divide the difficult spelling words, I had loved only Stephen Malone. The only trouble there was that he still considered me his little sister.

To complicate matters, through Edward's influence Stephen, too, decided that he would join the Salvation Army and use his life to serve God and humanity. He couldn't wait to come home and tell us.

"Stephen," said Papa, "God has been leading you all the while."

Mama turned her mist-filled blue eyes toward Papa. "Will, our prayers have been answered. Our Stephen has found himself at last."

"You were the ones who gave me a Christian home," Stephen replied simply. "That had a lot to do with my decision."

He turned to me. "Jenny," he said, "will you go for a walk in the garden with me?"

And so Stephen and I walked among the flowers, where June moonlight traced silvery shadows through the maple trees.

"For a time I considered the Presbyterian ministry," he disclosed after we had talked awhile. "Then I attended a Salvation Army meeting with Edward and began to feel that the Army is the right place for me. I like its down-to-earth manner in reaching out to help people. I like the method the Salvationists use as they travel in the marketplace and influence people in everyday situations—just as Jesus did. It has become a real call of God to me."

"Oh, Stephen," was all I could think to say.

"Jenny, a drinking man was converted at that meeting, and I saw how the Army fights the liquor problem. I want to play a role in lifting the fallen."

He stopped and in the moonlight glow I observed a sudden indefinable look in his eyes.

"Jenny, the man who accepted the Lord that day had read your story based on my mother's life. Your story, I'm sure, played a part in his conversion. It helped me also to reach my decision for the Army."

Looking up at Stephen, I realized abruptly that he hadn't called me his little sister for a long time. "Jenny," he said and reached for my hand.

With that Stephen opened his heart with words of love that every girl likes to hear. Together then we planned our work in the Salvation Army.

"I doubt if I'll ever be a Major or a Lieutenant Colonel, or accomplish great things as Edward will," Stephen reflected thoughtfully. "But, Jenny, you and I together may lead many to Christ. I'll do what I can, and you will witness through your writing, and in other ways."

After that we made plans at every opportunity. Then, one autumn day in Papa's garden Stephen made the request that started our careers as a life team together. "Do you mind if Jenny and I are married next month, Mr. Will?"

I smiled up at the handsome young man whom I had always loved. I turned to smile at Papa, who held Clayton's little girl on his lap.

"Little Sister," Papa murmured, and reached for my hand.

"Stephen," he said, looking up at the tall young captain in the Salvation Army uniform. "Stephen, my son."

# 15

# Papa's Graduation

Papa was looking forward to Jerry's graduation from medical school. There had been so many graduations in our family. They made us realize that the "nows" and "yesterdays" flow steadily like a mountain stream toward the tomorrows beckoning to new life channels.

"Each link in the life chain helps one to advance and live more fully," Papa reflected. "And graduations lead toward new achievements. Such milestone occasions make us stand upright and look tall in thought."

Papa had ever looked tall in thought, since he couldn't abide the idea of peering downward to view only the dirt and disappointments in life.

When the doctor said that Papa shouldn't attempt the trip for Jerry's graduation, naturally he was disappointed. It would be hard for him to remain at home while the rest attended, but remembering his philosophy, he accepted the news quietly. Two days later he suffered another heart attack.

Papa remained under the oxygen tent several days. He grew better then and was allowed to receive visitors. He read his Bible, books, and magazines. He witnessed daily to the visitors, nurses, doctors, and other patients.

"A hospital is the very place to weigh spiritual values," Papa commented. "So many people are embarrassed to discuss religion in the workaday world. But here . . ." His eyes for a brief moment held a faraway look as if he viewed distant horizons.

"Mr. Jennings," said the pretty, blue-eyed nurse, "it's time for your medicine."

"Young lady, you're just like my son Jerry, talking nothing but medicine."

"How many sons do you have?" asked the petite Marion Jaggers. "I've seen quite a few young men coming in to see you."

"I have four sons and one daughter," Papa replied proudly. He turned to me as I sat near his bed. "This is my Jenny," he said.

"The two tallest boys with the chestnut-brown hair are Clayton and John. Clayton teaches in a Presbyterian college and John is a Baptist minister. The auburn-haired boy with the bouncing, dramatic manner is my son Jim, a Methodist minister. Jerry, the youngest, is still in medical school."

Papa repressed the merest hint of a sigh. "He graduates next month."

"He must be the one with blonde hair and sea blue eyes," Miss Jaggers commented.

Papa looked keenly at the nurse. "Sea blue eyes, eh? Why, we hadn't defined the color in such precise terms."

Miss Jaggers lifted her own blue eyes. She reached for her medicine tray. "He's a handsome young man, as are your other sons," she said, smiling pleasantly.

"I have a son-in-law also," Papa said, "and his young brother is my son, too."

"What a relationship!" laughed the nurse. "Tell me about it sometime."

After she left, the faraway look appeared again in Papa's eyes. He lifted his hand to his chin in the old thoughtful gesture.

"Jenny, the three oldest boys fell in love at first sight, you know. Now about that young lady—somehow I have an intuition—"

I couldn't keep from smiling. "Oh, Papa, you and your intuitions!"

"Jenny, you're just like your mother. But like me, too," he added quietly, "I've given you the urge to write, if nothing else."

"I'm not sure about that, Papa. You see, I have received only rejections lately."

He looked keenly at me, as he had at the pretty nurse. "You've been too busy living, that's all. Getting married, caring for your husband, and now for little Stephen."

We both smiled tenderly when he spoke of our second Stephen. At 11 months, Stevie-boy was an exact replica of his father.

"Don't let the business of living hinder you long from being creative, though," Papa advised me. "I once had dreams of writing, too, remember. However, maybe I couldn't have created words after all, and the living was more important."

"Why, of course," I assured him. "Who else has lived a life so rich as yours and influenced so many people?"

"About your writing, Jenny," he said, "promise me you won't relinquish it. Go ahead and live deeply with your family. Grope diligently for the heart of people. Feel with them, share with them, and help when needed. You'll be able then to write what you have lived, as you share your faith and theirs with your readers."

"Oh, Papa, if only I could live and share my faith as you have! Why, when I think of how you've read your Bible and witnessed to the neighbors . . ."

"Milton Tanner used to think he didn't have a friend in the world," Papa reflected, his thin hands pleating a corner of the sheet.

"But you helped change his outlook and played a role in his conversion when you talked to him that snowy night. You helped win Uncle Pettigrew to the Lord also."

Papa's eyes almost twinkled. "Your Aunt Eliza gave him a push, too, you know."

"You started Sam Lightner reading the Bible," I recalled. "You helped Lem Bollen to relinquish drink. And what about helping Paul Trainer?" I asked, as I remembered their talks in the little lean-to room off our kitchen.

"Tony Kiśer will be the science teacher in our new high school," Papa said. "Hermann Kiser really grew interested in astronomy there in the Boys' Club. He read to Tony and taught him to watch the stars."

"Your silver dollar helped make Tony and our other young people what they are today," I said, as I remembered the 10 traits we cultivated in order to attain it.

"Uncle Ralph really had his problems," I recalled then. "Oh, Papa, every person we've known has had problems that made a story!"

"Problem stories in a community keep life revolving," Papa meditated "Our lives are linked together through them."

A ray of understanding flowed suddenly between us.

"I'll write despite everything," I promised then, determined to brush past rejections aside. "I'll write about our neighbors, Papa, and how Deep Valley lives have fitted together in patterns planned by God. If only I can convey the meaning of existence in the everyday episodes, and make my characters come alive for readers!"

Papa's eyes lighted briefly. "Little Sister . . ." he murmured, then paused without pursuing his thought.

"I'll write about you, Papa—and about Mama, and Clayton, and the others. I'll tell about the old Baptist church . . ."

"And the story of the new Sunday school, of course."

We spoke then about the varied religious leanings in our family and in the lives of our friends.

"The wondrous thing about the separate paths we have followed is that each one has sought a personal relationship with God—the same quest and the same ultimate goal."

Papa stared at the corner of the sheet. "Yes, Deep Valley character has cut its teeth on some tough experiences—floods, fires, failures and such—but also some happy times. The living experiences have molded our lives together; they've guided us in our quest for Christ. And in finding Him, we've found meaning to life and human relationships."

A contented, happy smile trailed over Papa's face as he looked out the window. "I'm glad that all of you except Jerry are established in your own homes. That pretty young nurse, now . . ." he mused once again.

Later I wondered if it were mere coincidence—or another of God's working in human relationships—that Marion Jaggers was on duty when Stephen and I called for help as Papa grew worse that night. She came and efficiently took charge.

"Jerry—" Papa spoke drowsily after his shot.

A few hours later he aroused. "I hear music," he said softly.

Stephen and I looked at each other. We heard no earthly music in the hospital.

Yet Papa repeated softly, "I hear music." His voice, as always, was one of appreciation for any beauty he beheld or heard.

"Betsey," he murmured, "I'd give anything in the world to be at home with you again."

Stephen and I shared glances once more. Mama herself had been sick all week. Nellie Bender, who had stayed with Mama and Papa since my marriage, was caring for her.

"Daddy Lovell is sick, I tell you," Papa spoke positively. "I must go to him." And a bit later, "The Tanners may be needing apples, Betsey."

The nurse stood close. "Jerry," said Papa.

At the foot of the bed I whispered to Stephen, "Surely we're not imagining things, but every time she appears he calls for Jerry."

"His intuition," Stephen said simply.

When Jerry came the next day it was love at first sight—as with the other boys—on being introduced to Marion. She attended his graduation with us, and they were married the next year.

Now, however, in the hospital room that night Papa himself was graduating to the supreme sphere of life.

"I hear music," he repeated softly.

He attempted to lift his right hand to his chin in the familiar thoughtful gesture, as if contemplating the everlasting music.

"The neighbors—may be needing—apples, Betsey," he murmured.

With that Papa graduated into glory.